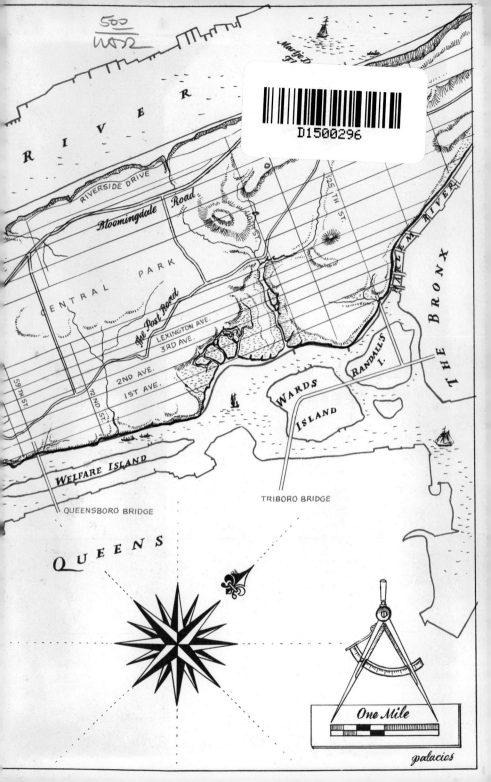

BATTLE FOR MANHATTAN

BATTLE FOR MANHATTAN

by

BRUCE BLIVEN, Jr.

Illustrated with Photographs

❧❧

HENRY HOLT AND COMPANY
NEW YORK

For My Parents

BATTLE FOR MANHATTAN

I

FROM the time the British realized that their trouble with the American colonies might involve them in a war of major proportions, New York City, above all other American cities, was where they wanted to be. The Hudson River, rather than the charm of the town proper, was New York's great attraction; for the Hudson, leading almost to Lake George, which led to Lake Champlain, which emptied into the Richelieu River, which emptied into the St. Lawrence, suggested an obvious line, dotted with water, to be held. The idea of separating New England from the rest of the colonies and dividing the American effort in two was a prime object of British strategy.

New York had more to offer General Sir William Howe, the commander of the British army, than its position at the Hudson's mouth. Since the city was on an island surrounded by navigable waters, and since the British navy was strong while an American navy did not exist, New York appealed as a base of operations that could be guarded, almost literally, by sea power

alone. The town itself, a pleasant, growing agglomer-
ation of old Dutch and new English buildings with a
peacetime population of about twenty thousand, was on
the southernmost tip of Manhattan. Howe wanted suitable quarters for his troops during the months ahead,
and he was more interested in the city than in the rest
of the island, the rolling, well-watered, and generously
wooded countryside north of the built-up area, where
many wealthy New Yorkers owned farms or country
estates.

Howe imagined, furthermore, that he might get help,
and perhaps hospitality as well, from those New Yorkers
who wanted the British to win the war. It was hard to
say just how many they were, but certainly there had
been more Tories than Whigs among the city's large
property holders at the beginning of the conflict; and
many of the less well-to-do residents, including govern-
ment officials and employees, lesser merchants and the
Episcopal clergy, agreed with the gentry.

By the summer of 1776 Boston, which had seemed
so important in 1775, was almost forgotten. Boston was
in American hands, and Bostonians, along with all other
Americans sympathetic to the revolutionary cause, were
still speaking excitedly about the stirring events that
had taken place at Concord, Lexington, and Bunker's
Hill—and about the siege that had finally forced the
British to leave Boston in March, 1776. But nearly all
Americans had believed a year or so earlier that the
fighting around Boston would decide the war one way
or another and bring some sort of peace. No one

thought so any longer, of course. The British had simply become involved at Boston, had been beaten there,
and had retired to Halifax for the purpose of coming
back, at least five times stronger, to attack at a more
profitable place.

Only a few patriots had considered, or had dared
mention, the possibility that the American army, commanded by General George Washington, might be too
feeble to hold New York. The decision to defend it had
been made painlessly because the alternative was at first
very nearly unthinkable. New York's fortifications had
been begun in February, before the British left Boston;
and an enormous effort had been spent on the construc-
tion of forts, redoubts, barricades, gun emplacements,
and trenches. But because there was so much to fortify—
both sides of both rivers in addition to the key terrain
features all over the long, narrow, rocky island of Manhattan—none of the works was first class and most of
them were pitifully inadequate. The Americans were
short of military engineers, just as they were short of
all kinds of officer talent, and they had to copy most of
their plans out of military textbooks, an expedient which
could hardly be compared with custom-designing a
strongpoint to fit its site. The forts were made of sod,
and most of the trenches lacked suitable breastworks. In
a few cases the fortifications were almost worse than
nothing. An embankment along the southern shore of the
island was an example: it was mostly scrap lumber
(spars, logs, and pieces of demolished wharves), but
its chinks had been filled in with broken bottles, rocks,

and bits of assorted junk which were likely to become
—under bombardment by British warships—about as
dangerous as the shells themselves.

A considerable part of the whole effort to get New
York ready for the enemy's assault was calculated to
frustrate the British navy. The Americans hoped, in
part, to substitute shore batteries for the warships they
lacked; they thought that with guns on Governor's Island
and on the Brooklyn-Queens shore, as well as on the
Manhattan shore, they could make the East River too
dangerous for the British sailors; and they believed
that the Hudson could be blocked off by sinking a line
of heavily weighted ships' hulls across it just a few
hundred yards north of where the George Washington
Bridge now stands. Such a line had been started in June,
with pointed timbers mounted on top of the sunken
ships. It was not by any means an impassable obstruc-
tion; the underwater obstacles were supposed to worry
the British captains, while gunfire from the American
batteries at Fort Lee, on the New Jersey end of the
line, and Fort Washington, on the Manhattan side,
added to their discouragement. The combination might
make the British feel that a sail up the river was not
worth the risk involved.

While the work was going on, and as long as there
was still time to make improvements, Washington and
his council of principal officers managed to maintain an
unrealistic optimism about the shape of events to come.
The Continental Congress in Philadelphia, far enough
away to have its hopes protected from the realities of

things in New York, was far more sanguine than the
Commander-in-Chief. And he was elaborately deferen-
tial to Congress' puffed-up view of American capabilities—not because it flattered him but because he believed strongly that the leader of the country's army
ought to be subservient to its legislature.

Even the arrival of the British in late June and early
July had failed to impress the hopeful Americans to
anything like a reasonable degree. It was the largest
expeditionary force Great Britain had ever assembled:
approximately thirty-two thousand well-trained professional soldiers, completely armed and equipped, sup-
ported by a fleet that included ten ships of the line,
twenty frigates, and something like one hundred and
seventy transports of various sizes. There were so many
masts in the lower harbor, south of Staten Island, where
the British had promptly set up their camp, that the bay
looked to one observer like a forest of pine trees with
their branches trimmed. And almost as soon as they had
arrived, on July 12th, the captains of two of the British
frigates, the *Phoenix* and the *Rose,* showed what they
thought of the American attempts to deny them the use
of the Hudson. Taking advantage of a fresh breeze and
a favorable tide, and accompanied by two tenders, they
swept past the shore batteries and up the river. They
sailed through the Fort Lee-Fort Washington line of
obstructions and all the way to Tappan Bay, thirty miles
upstream, near Tarrytown. On the night of August 16th
a pathetic assortment of American small craft tried to
set fire to them and failed. Two days later the ships re-

turned to the harbor, running in the opposite direction
past all the same hazards, without suffering appreciable
damage—and as if they regarded the Hudson as their
own private stream.

At the end of August, moving with a self-confidence
rather like that of the captains of the *Phoenix* and the
Rose, Howe seized the western end of Long Island, including Brooklyn and Queens. The Americans were outmaneuvered and outfought, and in eight days the first
part of the British capture of New York was complete.
It was only then that the Americans saw what might
have been evident long before: Howe had enough power
to take New York more or less as he chose. And that
being the case, it seemed logical—at least to Major
General Nathanael Greene and several other of Washington's advisers—that New York City should be
burned to the ground. "Two thirds of the property of
the city of New York and the suburbs," Green wrote,
"belong to the Tories. We have no very great reason
to run any risk for its defense." And burning the city,
he pointed out, would "deprive the enemy of an opportunity of barracking their whole army together. . . ."

But the thought of destroying New York, especially
after months of believing that New York could be de-
fended, was too shocking for Congress. Evacuation of
the city was in itself a demoralizing idea, and only after
twelve days of intermittent debate—while precious time
was lost—could Washington's Council of War bring
itself to approve the withdrawal that was unavoidable.

More clearly than anyone else, George Washington

realized the wretched condition of his army. During the
second week in September, while he waited for Howe to
move against New York City itself, the General found
himself in a dreadful dilemma, which was partly of his
own making but no less baffling on that account. It is
hard to imagine that any of the crises he had to face
later on—and there were to be a good many of them—
was more difficult to bear.

The General saw that by leaving his army on Manhattan Island he was putting it in grave jeopardy. As
the *Phoenix* and the *Rose* had demonstrated, the British
fleet was capable of taking an assault force up the
Hudson to land almost anywhere north of his forces.
A landing on the Westchester shore of Long Island
Sound was equally possible, perhaps even easier. And if
Howe made either move or a combination of both, he
could trap the Americans, cutting them off from any possible retreat, and defeat them in his own good time. By
staying, in short, Washington risked total disaster.

Yet he intended to stay. He intended to take that risk
for one appallingly simple reason: he estimated that
after their defeat on Long Island his troops were too
demoralized to stand a major retreat. The losses there
had been fairly heavy—something more than a thousand
men, most of whom had been taken prisoner—but they
were far less serious than the damage done to the American army's self-esteem. As soon as the troops had got-
ten back from Brooklyn to Manhattan (a withdrawal
under cover of darkness that had been by far their most
successful maneuver of the battle), Washington's mili-

tiamen had started to desert. They had just disappeared, walking out of their camps and taking off for their homes. In some cases whole regiments had vanished, almost as a body. Within a week, for example, the eight thousand men in thirteen Connecticut militia regiments had become two thousand.

Most of those who had deserted were short-enlistment men, drafted by their states for emergencies of just a few months at a time—the so-called "Continental militia"—and they were the poorest trained soldiers in the army. The worst of it was that in many cases the soldiers who remained were about as discouraged as the ones who had picked up and gone home. The militiamen's attitude had to some extent infected the minds of the longer-term enlistees. That had not been hard to do, since so many of the militiamen's complaints had been no less than plain truth.

The deserters said that the officers were incompetent, and quite a few of them were. They complained about the food, the supplies, and the lack of weapons. They were right: Washington's procurement and supply system was in wretched shape. They said that the General himself didn't know what he was doing, and that the war was as good as lost. The deserters were wrong, but not entirely and not by very far.

Long Island had been Washington's first battle (as compared with the Boston siege), and there was no way in which he could escape the responsibility and the blame for the series of errors that had been made there, both in the planning and in the fighting; and earlier he had been guilty of thinking, along with Congress and nearly everyone else, that the war would be short. (A mistake which had led to blunders in recruiting, in setting the length of enlistments, and in obtaining supplies.)

But the war was not quite lost. And Washington's army, despite the low state of its morale, was still some distance from breaking up under the weight of disillusion. There was one chance, the General thought, that his troops' spirits could be lifted. Not by the long retreat to the comparatively safe ground of Westchester, for that might only make matters worse by emphasizing the demoralizing fact that Howe was the master of the situation. But by a successful battle, however small, which could prove to the satisfaction of his soldiers that the British were something less than invincible.

II

THE British invasion of Manhattan started on the morning of September 15, 1776. The day was a Sunday, and it was bright and clear at first, but too hot and muggy to be really pleasant; the weather was more appropriate to July or early August than to the middle of September. Washington, who was up at dawn, had spent the night in a new headquarters, the elegant Roger Morris house, now known as the Jumel Mansion, which still stands at 161st Street on the brink of Coogan's Bluff, overlooking the Polo Grounds. From its front portico, looking south, Washington could see Harlem, a small Dutch settlement then more than a hundred years old on the low flats beside the Harlem River, in the vicinity of what is now 125th Street.

From the distant vantage point the whole Harlem area appeared surprisingly quiet. Still, Washington was almost certain that the British were going to attack there before the day was over. He expected them to move from Queens in force and use Buchanan's (now Ward's) Island and Montresor's (now Randall's) Is-

18

land, which were both in their hands, as steppingstones. For several days General Howe had been building up to an assault at Harlem without any noticeable effort to conceal his choice of the site, and Washington had no reason to think that the enemy preparations were misleading.

To begin with, British ships had been sailing boldly up the East River from the lower harbor, ignoring frenzied but erratic gunfire from the American batteries on the Manhattan shore; some ships had ventured as far north as Hell Gate, just south of Buchanan's and Montresor's islands, and presumably, when the time came, they would support the Harlem landing with fire from their cannon. Furthermore, Howe had assembled a considerable number of flat-bottomed landing barges— big, sixteen-oared rowboats, each capable of carrying fifty or sixty men—in coves and inlets along the Long Island side of the river, many of them in the mouth of Newtown Creek. They were the same boats that he had used with conspicuous success on August 22nd to ferry his troops from Staten Island to Gravesend Bay, between what are now Fort Hamilton and Coney Island, for the invasion of Long Island. Moreover the British had gone to considerable trouble trying to knock out the nine-gun American battery at Horn's Hook, the point of land at the northern end of what has since become Carl Schurz Park, near Eighty-ninth Street and East End Avenue. British ships had fired at the battery as they sailed past, and Howe's artillerists had attempted to hit it with field artillery shooting across the river from the Queens

shore. They had had no success whatever, but their
motive seemed clear: the Horn's Hook battery was in a
fairly good position to interfere with an assault on
Harlem by shelling the landing craft or dueling with the
supporting warships. Finally, to make the picture complete, Howe's troops had been reported on the move;
before dark on the previous day, Saturday, three or four
thousand British soldiers, according to Washington's
lookouts, had marched down to the Queens shore, and
some of them—although no one knew how many—had
been ferried across to Montresor's Island.

Even though the British preparations had moved
slowly, Washington's defense was anything but ready.
He had several of his strongest units, including Smallwood's Marylanders and Knowlton's Rangers, in position at the Harlem section of the East River shoreline
ready to meet the British assault boats, but his force as
a whole was shockingly vulnerable. It was scattered
about the island in such a way that perhaps half its potential power was unusable. The army was off balance,
and it needed at least another day or two before it
could be pulled together—time it was not going to be
allowed.

The main trouble was that Washington was still in
the midst of shifting his troops. Although the British
certainly did not realize what was going on, he was in the
process of surrendering the prize—the city of New York
—that Howe intended to seize by force.

If Howe's methodical mounting of his assault had

taken perhaps forty-eight hours longer, New York
would have been his for just the occupying. Washington's men were getting out of it as fast as they could,
evacuating their stores of supplies and their sick and
wounded. Their fastest had been painfully slow, for the
army was short of wagons as well as horses.

Washington had not started the retreat until the previous Thursday, September 12th—and only after Congress had given him permission to leave New York if he
thought it necessary. Washington's revised plan called
for the massing of nearly his entire strength on the generally high ground north of what is now 125th Street, a
rocky plateau called Harlem Heights. Its southern
boundary ran an irregular course across Manhattan
from the Harlem to the Hudson, and it was protected
by an almost unbroken line of steep bluffs, some up to
sixty feet tall. Washington hoped that his army, for all
its shortcomings and weaknesses, would be able to defend those bluffs and keep the British off that plateau.

But unfortunately, as of Sunday morning, half of
Washington's twenty thousand men were still occupied,
in one capacity or another, south of the Harlem Heights
stronghold. Five thousand of them, commanded by General Israel Putnam, were in and around the city of New
York. Some were guarding the line of fortifications that
protected the city on the north, and that ran from what
is now the foot of Grand Street (two blocks south of
the Williamsburg Bridge) on the East River to Vestry
Street (four blocks south of the Holland Tunnel) on
the Hudson. Some were loading up the last of the food,

ammunition, tents, camp kettles, and other stores. The
other five thousand were strung out in a thin line along
the shore of the East River, from the city to Harlem, to
protect the one road that ran the full length of Manhattan, the escape route to the north. As Washington
fully realized, his stretched-out troop formation in-
vited defeat. If Howe landed anywhere between the
city and the Heights, cracked through the fragile line of
river guards, and then marched due west to the Hudson, he might easily cut off a third or perhaps a full half
of the American army. The chances were that he would
have won the war then and there.

At about nine o'clock Washington mounted his horse
and—with a small party of the aides who accompanied
him to transmit orders, collect information, and assist
in the management of a battle—set out from the Morris
house down the Post Road in the direction of Harlem.
However anxious he might be at times, the General
almost always looked as if he had everything under control, especially when he was on horseback; he was one
of the country's best horsemen—the very best, according to Thomas Jefferson—and he sat easily and grace-
fully in the saddle. In addition Washington had natural
presence, in the theatrical sense. He was a big man—six
feet two inches tall and weighing around two hundred
and ten pounds—and he took possession of a situation
as effortlessly as a great actor takes possession of a
stage. Washington was forty-four years old. Except for
a lot of trouble with his teeth, which he was gradually

exchanging for false ones, his health was excellent. He was full of energy, and he was unusually strong. On the rare occasions when there was time for recreation of any sort, he and the headquarters officers used to see how far they could throw a heavy iron bar—a game rather like shot-putting. It tested their arm, shoulder, and back muscles in particular, and Washington could outtoss his aides, some of whom were in their early twenties, without half trying. He had a long, full face with round, high cheekbones, a firm chin, and a wide mouth. His nose was large, but long and straight rather than prominent. He wore his dark brown hair, which was usually powdered, in a queue, pulled straight back from his high forehead and tied with a ribbon at the nape of his neck, leaving puffs of fullness over his ears. His complexion, which bore the marks of an attack of smallpox he had suffered when he was nineteen, was naturally pale and had a kind of translucent quality, but it was now ruddy from exposure to the elements; it sunburned quickly but did not tan. His blue-gray eyes were set far apart beneath heavy, overhanging brows.

Washington's characteristic expression was one of good-natured reserve, and it was faintly self-conscious, partly because his teeth bothered him and partly because he habitually restrained his facial muscles in a deliberate effort to avoid showing how he felt or what he was thinking. He never threw himself on the mercy of his associates in a burst of unguarded frankness. He looked people straight in the eye, and he spoke up clearly, although his voice was generally rather low. But he was almost always controlled or withholding, and sometimes this reserve was taken for hostility, which it was not. When Washington intended to be hard, and moved from his normal dignified caution into icy, impenetrable formality, there was no doubt what his mood was.

Washington was capable, furthermore, of getting angry enough to blow up completely. Not many of his friends or fellow officers were aware that, on occasion, his passionate temper might boil out of control, for he had struggled his whole life to keep it from doing so. Most of them had seen nothing worse than Washington in a stiff, correct freeze—and that in itself was rare. Yet beyond what most of his associates thought was the General's angriest, there was another degree; there was the possibility that his normally placid features might become contorted with rage, and that he would bellow wild curses, waving his arms and stamping furiously. Washington, who of course knew it could happen, dreaded the thought.

His uniform was blue and buff. His blue coat was beautifully tailored; because there was almost no padding beneath the shoulders, the gold epaulets sat low, and the coat followed the body's natural lines instead of being squared off. It had swallowtails, which came to his knees but were buttoned up for riding, and wide buff lapels, which buttoned back in place, that went the full length of the coat. His long vest and narrow breeches were buff, too. He wore black riding boots with spurs, and a black, three-cornered hat, an ordinary low-

crowned, wide-brimmed civilian hat but with its brim
stitched to the crown in back and at both sides near the
temples. Washington's hat differed from those of his
aides in only one way—the color of the cockade on the
front of its brim. It was black, which showed that he
was a general officer. A light-blue ribbon worn diagonally across his chest, over his vest, indicated that he was
a full general. The cockade-and-ribbon system was the
equivalent of modern shoulder or collar insignia, and
it was necessary because the army had no uniform; one
could tell that a man was an American officer by the
cockade in his hat—green for lieutenants, yellow or buff
for captains, and pink or red for field grade officers.
Major generals and brigadier generals, in addition to
their black cockades, wore pink ribbons across their
chests, and generals' aides wore green ones. Otherwise
there was no certainty or system except, in some cases,
within regiments, and as many men were fighting in
civilian clothes which they themselves had supplied as
were in uniforms of any kind. Washington wanted all
the members of his immediate staff, his headquarters
group or "family" as it was called, to get buff-and-blue
uniforms like his own, but not all of them had had time
or an opportunity to do so.

Washington's party rode down from the Heights'
high ground to the plains below through a draw, a long
hill where St. Nicholas Avenue now descends from 154th
Street to 141st Street—the one real break in the otherwise abrupt southern rim of the plateau. The Post Road,
running south, kept close to the base of the bluffs for

the next half mile or so, just as St. Nicholas Avenue
does now. (The elephantine granite boulders of the pali-
sades are still on view in St. Nicholas Park, just east of
the City College campus.) At about what is now 131st
Street and St. Nicholas Avenue, Washington and his
aides turned off the Post Road onto a secondary road
which led southeast across the plains to Harlem and
the Harlem River. From the little village—a handful of
buildings, including a town hall and a church, which, if
it were still standing, would be just west of First Avenue, between 124th and 125th Streets—the British soldiers on Buchanan's and Montresor's islands were
plainly visible in their scarlet uniforms as they moved
about among the trees near the water. But the scene remained curiously peaceful; there was no sign of the landing boats, and there were not as many warships in the
upper East River as there had been at dark the evening
before. Washington was relieved; every additional hour
gave the soldiers in the city a better chance to finish the
evacuation.

But the lack of British activity in the Harlem area
was misleading. Although Washington had not yet
heard about it, ominous developments had taken place
farther south on both the Hudson and the East rivers.
Earlier in the morning, three British men-of-war—the
Renown, the *Repulse,* and the *Pearl*—had sailed up the
Hudson from a position off Greenwich, just north of the
city, to the small harbor known as Striker's Bay on the
west side of the island at about what is now Ninety-
sixth Street. Despite all the changes in the shoreline

since then, one can still see a suggestion of the bay's outline; the ground slopes down from all sides to form a kind of bowl, and Riverside Drive swings inland and over a viaduct to avoid taking a pronounced dip. These ships presented the possibility of a diversionary, if minor, British landing on the Hudson side of Manhattan, which was practically undefended; even a handful of British soldiers would have been able to make quite a nuisance of themselves there, and it was just as well that, since he didn't know about the *Renown,* the *Repulse,* and the *Pearl,* Washington did not have that threat to add to his other worries.

The activity in the East River had graver implications. During the night five British warships—the frigates that had been expected to support the Harlem attack—had sailed down to Kip's Bay, a modest indentation in the Manhattan shore at about what is now the foot of East Thirty-fourth Street, and had moved into the cove. The Americans guarding the Kip's Bay shore had heard them drop anchor, and during the hours of darkness had exchanged bantering insults with the British sailors aboard them.

At daybreak it appeared that the ships had not come merely for conversation. They were anchored, bow to stern, in a line about as close to the rocky shore as they could get—not more than two hundred yards away— and their cannon had been rolled out through the gun ports into firing position. The *Roebuck,* on the north end of the line, and the *Phoenix,* on the south, were the largest of the five, with forty guns apiece. The *Orpheus,* next to the *Roebuck,* had thirty-two; then came the *Carysfort* with twenty-eight, and the *Rose,* with thirty-two. A full broadside, as the Kip's Bay defenders could easily count, would add up to eighty-six guns. By British navy standards, the ships were fairly small. The *Eagle* and the *Asia,* in the lower harbor, were sixty-four-gun warships and half a dozen of the other British vessels in the fleet at New York boasted fifty guns; yet considered as floating, massed artillery—which was how the soldiers on shore regarded them—the five frigates looked alarmingly powerful, and they seemed huge, as any ship does when it is seen close to the shore. Their masts and rigging towered into the air, and the rounded sides of their black hulls, which were banded with white, appeared to be bristling with fire power.

The soldiers confronted by this sight were overawed without knowing exactly what to make of it. They would have been terrified if they had realized that Kip's Bay, rather than Harlem, had become the target for Howe's assault, and that the five warships were in position for the naval bombardment that was to precede the landing of the first troops. Howe had originally intended to land at Harlem, as Washington surmised, but he had been obliged to change his mind; the waters around the islands at Hell Gate were much more treacherous in those days than they are now (the worst obstructions have been removed and the channels have been dredged), and the captains of the ships in the British East River task force were loath to approach the Harlem shore. At the last moment, rather than try to land without the support of the frigates' gunfire, Howe had changed his objective to Kip's Bay.

The shift in plan disturbed him little, if at all. Howe was confident that if he could get his regiments ashore in good order at almost any point, he could capture the city without serious difficulty; one starting place was about as good as another. Kip's Bay, in addition to being easily navigable, offered a large, open, V-shaped meadow rising from the shore between two brooks that almost met as they emptied into the river—a good battlefield that provided hardly any cover or concealment for the defending Americans and would make a fine place for the British troops to assemble. Furthermore, there was no American artillery to dispute a Kip's Bay landing— nothing comparable to the disputatious battery at Horn's Hook. And finally there was the tactical advantage of surprise in changing to Thirty-fourth Street after all the undisguised preparations for a 125th Street assault; the earlier build-up, which had been in earnest, now served as a confusing feint.

For the time being, there was nothing the Americans along the Kip's Bay shore could do except look at the British warships and wonder, anxiously, what was about to happen. The ships' crews were merely standing by, and there was not much sense in the Americans' opening fire in the face of the naval guns; even at the short range, their muskets were entirely inadequate and could only provoke a devastating reply. So, as the bright sun continued to rise in the sky and the morning grew warmer, the soldiers simply sat in their trenches—a series of shallow ditches with no breastworks except the loose earth tossed up on the river side in digging them— waiting and growing more worried every moment.

In so precarious a spot first-class troops might have been demoralized to the point of panic, and the men at Kip's Bay, who were in Colonel William Douglas' Connecticut brigade, were nearly all raw recruits. Some of them had been in the army less than a week and had barely begun to get acquainted with the other soldiers in their companies; they were still wearing the clothes they had brought from home, and those lucky enough to have any arms at all carried their families' muskets. (In place of firearms, some carried pikes of a homemade variety—a pickax or a scythe blade hammered straight and fastened to a pole.) These newest men had not been issued any equipment or given any training, and most of them had been brought up in peaceful Connecticut towns, remote from the frontier, where they had not had much chance to pick up experience even as irregulars; they were hardly more than civilians under military jurisdiction, and soldiers in only a legal sense.

One of the four regiments in Douglas' brigade was considerably more competent than the other three—it ranked as fair to middling, while the others were only "Continental militia." Unluckily, the fair-to-middling outfit was stationed on the south end of Douglas' section of the East River line, and the warships were at his left, on the north, where he had posted some of his greenest soldiers.

A brigade, on paper, looked sizable enough. The full

strength of Douglas' outfit was one hundred and forty
officers and thirteen hundred enlisted men, but hardly a
third of these were on hand and ready to fight. More
than five hundred were sick; like nearly a quarter of
Washington's entire army, they were unfit for combat
on account of a fever brought on, it was believed, by
drinking polluted water. During its shore-guard duty,
moreover, the brigade had been divided into two sec-
tions, or reliefs, which took twelve-hour turns watching
the river around the clock; on Sunday morning, as a
matter of routine, only half its effective strength was in
the trenches—a total of not more than four hundred
and fifty officers and men. To be sure, the men off duty
were not far away. They were camped in the woods
nearby or wandering around the vicinity trying to find
something to eat or drink. While they should have come
running in an emergency, rounding them up was difficult; and for hours the ominous presence of the five frigates, which were not making a sound, was not defined
as an emergency.

The men who were in position in the trenches had
been on duty all night. They were tired. What was perhaps worse from a morale standpoint, they were fam-
ished, because no rations had been issued for twenty-
four hours. All in all, the Kip's Bay defense was in
sorry condition.

Although one might think the brigade's commander
was at fault, Colonel Douglas had already proved his
excellence as a leader. His reputation was very high;
and, in fact, he had been given the brigade less than two

weeks earlier partly as a reward for his fine work at
the head of a battalion during the Battle of Long Island. He was a tall, straight, thirty-three-year-old veteran of the French and Indian War, and a versatile,
experienced fighter. Clearly, he had not been in charge
of his outfit long enough to have much influence on his
troops one way or another, still less to make soldiers
out of them. The brigade's other troubles were matters
far beyond his control. He had had no warning, of
course, of the change in Howe's assault plans; so that
when he found himself, with as feeble a unit as any in
the entire army, squarely in the path of a high-powered,
well-disciplined, and wholly unexpected British attack,
it was simply a case of spectacularly bad luck.

Colonel Douglas did the one thing possible at this
last moment: he tried to shift more of his men to the
northern end of his line, moving them up, within the
trenches, toward his left. But as time passed and nothing
happened, his troops were hardly inspired with fighting
spirit; they thought very little of offering themselves as
targets for the British gunners, and the longer they
thought about it the less their enthusiasm grew. One
sixteen-year-old New Haven recruit, Joseph Martin,
who was frightened and bored in about equal measure,
came across a litter of commercial papers on the floor
of a shed close to his post. He sat down on a barrel and
to pass the time began to study them, trying to figure
out just what they were all about.

Douglas' trenches followed the contours of the bay
in an irregular line, as close to the edge of the river as

George Washington, by Charles Willson Peale (1778).
(Courtesy of Pennsylvania Academy of the Fine Arts)

Plan of the City of New York, by Bernard Ratzer. Surveyed in 1767.
(Stokes Collection, New York Public Library)

Sir William Howe, a mezzotint by an anonymous British artist.
(Spencer Collection, New York Public Library)

A view of New York from the North West, from the *Atlantic Neptune.* An aquatint, of about 1772, by Joseph F. W. Des Barres. The churches, from left to right, are Trinity, the Lutheran, the Middle Dutch, the Wall Street Presbyterian, the French Church du St. Esprit, and the South Dutch Church. The Fort and Governor's House at the right. (Edward W. C. Arnold Collection, courtesy of Museum of the City of New York)

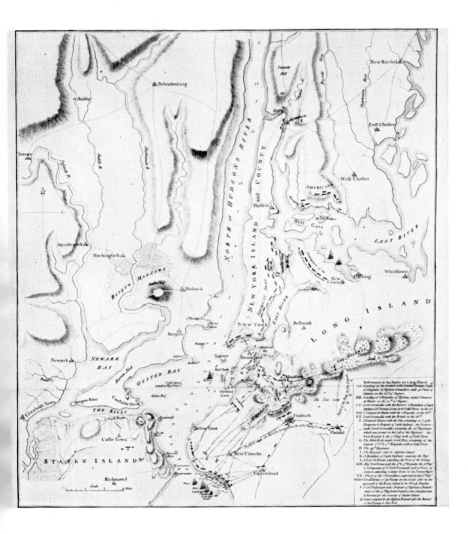

*A Plan of New York Island, with Part of Long Island, Staten Island &
East New Jersey, with a Particular Description of the Engagement on
the Woody Heights of Long Island, between Flatbush and Brooklyn,
on the 27th of August 1776.* (The Howe War Plan.) (Stokes Collection, New York Public Library)

A South East View of the City of New York in North America, by Captain Thomas Howdell of the Royal Artillery, engraved by P. Canot. Published in 1768. The large building was King's College (Columbia University) on the site now bounded by Murray, Barclay, Church, and Chapel streets; the palm tree was an invention, probably the engraver's. (Edward W. C. Arnold Collection, courtesy of Museum of the City of New York)

New York, With the Entrance of the North and East Rivers, from the Atlantic Neptune. (About 1773.) (J. Clarence Davies Collection, courtesy of Museum of the City of New York)

These are two of five views of New York Harbor and the vicinity published on one sheet in a collection of charts, plans, and views drawn and engraved by Joseph F. W. Des Barres and published by the Admiralty for the use of the Royal Navy.

The Narrows (Between Red and Yellow Hook, on Long Island, & The East Bluff, of Staten Island,) Bearing S.b.W., from the Atlantic Neptune. (About 1773.) (J. Clarence Davies Collection, courtesy of Museum of the City of New York)

18th June 1776, by Archibald Robertson. Captain Archibald Robertson, an engineer officer with British headquarters and deputy quartermaster general, sketched some of the ships of the British fleet as they lay below Staten Island. (Spencer Collection, New York Public Library)

View of the Narrows between Long Island & Staten Island, with our Fleet at Anchor & Lord Howe coming in (12th July 1776), by Archibald Robertson. (Spencer Collection, New York Public Library)

Taken from the heights above the watering place (*12 July 1776*), by Archibald Robertson. New York from Staten Island, with the *Phoenix* and the *Rose* sailing past the city's batteries in the far distance. (Spencer Collection, New York Public Library)

The Phoenix and the Rose Engaged by the Enemy's Fire Ships and Galleys on the 16 August, 1776, from a sketch by Sir James Wallace. The first naval print of the Revolutionary War period that shows American ships, if only fire ships, in action. (Stokes Collection, New York Public Library)

View of the North River from a Sloop, by Archibald Robertson.
(Spencer Collection, New York Public Library)

View of Morisinia (10 October 1777), by Archibald Robertson. From high ground close to McGown's Pass, with Harlem Meer, the Harlem Plains, the Harlem River and Montresor's and Buchanan's islands visible. (Spencer Collection, New York Public Library)

View of Harlem (1765), from *Valentine's Manual.* (J. Clarence Davies Collection, courtesy of Museum of the City of New York)

View of Hell Gate, by W. A. Williams. (1777) From Horn's Hook, near the north end of the present Carl Schurz Park, looking toward what is now Ward's Island. (J. Clarence Davies Collection, courtesy of Museum of the City of New York)

W A Williams del 1772

| Ioorn's Hook . | 3 Hancock's Rock . | 5 Morrisena . | 7 Pinfolds Place . | 9 The Pot . | 11 The Frying |
| The Gridiron . | 4 The Mill Rock . | 6 Bahannas Island . | 8 Hallet's Point . | 10 The Hogs back . | Pan . |

View of the Rebel Work round Walton's House, by Archibald Robertson. The Horn's Hook fortifications. (Spencer Collection, New York Public Library)

Opening of our battery at Hell Gate (8th September 1776), by Archibald Robertson. The British batteries shooting from Hallet's Point at Sargent's battery at Horn's Hook, across the East River. (Spencer Collection, New York Public Library)

it was practicable to dig them. Kip's Bay has been completely filled in by now, but then, at the deepest part of its bite into the shoreline, the water reached to between First and Second avenues on Thirty-fourth Street. The cove was a little less than a city block deep, and it ran from what is now Thirty-second Street to about Thirty-eighth Street, with a small promontory, like a widow's peak, jutting out from the shore near the center of the crescent, at about Thirty-fifth Street. Back of this promontory—a hundred feet east of Second Avenue on Thirty-fifth Street—stood the old Kip farmhouse, belonging to a family that had lived there for more than a century. Behind it was the meadow Howe expected to use as an assembly area. The ground rose gradually at first and then quite abruptly to a flat-topped hill called Inclenberg, now known as Murray Hill, which was owned by a wealthy Quaker merchant, Robert Murray. On Inclenberg's crest stood Murray's handsome country house, which was only twelve years old in 1776; if it were still standing, it would straddle Park Avenue between Thirty-sixth and Thirty-seventh streets. It was surrounded by gardens, lawns, orchards, and cultivated fields, the center of an estate which, while not particularly large, was a showplace—conspicuously placed, and with a lovely view, especially to the south and the east— that combined elegance with productivity.

There were only a few other houses, besides the Kip farm and the Murray mansion, in the Kip's Bay vicinity. One was the extensive John Watts place on the southwest of the open meadow. It was called Rose Hill Farm,

and the main house, at the end of a long, straight driveway flanked by geometrically precise orchards, was at
what is now Twenty-fourth Street, slightly west of
Second Avenue; most of the wooded area where Douglas' relief troops were camping was on Watts property.
Right on the river, at about Twenty-fifth Street, there
was a handsome house, called Bellevue, that belonged
to the Keteltas family. The Beekman mansion and one
or two other houses were to the north, and Turtle Bay
at Forty-sixth and Forty-seventh streets, rather than
Kip's Bay, was their focal point.

Just to the south of Inclenberg, from Park Avenue
almost to Lexington Avenue and between Thirty-first
and Thirty-second streets, there was a charming spring-
fed lake, four hundred feet long and perhaps half that
wide, called Sunfish Pond; the outlet brook from the
lake was one of the streams that meandered through
the meadow and emptied into Kip's Bay. The Post
Road, which was the island's main north-south thorough-
fare and the only one that extended the whole way from
New York to King's Bridge (which provided the exit
to the Bronx at the northern end of the island), ran
past the eastern bank of Sunfish Pond; and stagecoach
teams, stopping at the stone two and a half miles from
the city, often watered there.

From a military point of view the Post Road was the
island's key highway; it was Washington's evacuation
route and, in Howe's plans, one of the first objectives
to be seized. The Post Road headed north from the
city, along what is now the Bowery, to the present Astor

Place; there it veered slightly to the west, following the
course Broadway now takes, to Twenty-third Street. At
that point there was an important fork. The Post Road
turned to the northeast and the Bloomingdale Road,
the left-hand branch of the fork, went northwest. The
Bloomingdale Road marked out almost exactly the fu-
ture path of Broadway as far as 106th Street, where,
instead of turning north as Broadway does, it ran
straight ahead to the northwest for nine blocks and
came to a dead end at a farm owned by a family named
Hoaglandt at 115th Street and Riverside Drive. The
Post Road, cutting diagonally across the present grid of
streets, went from Twenty-third Street and Broadway
to Thirty-first Street and Lexington Avenue, past Sun-.
fish Pond and across a bridge over its outlet brook.
Then, following the course of Lexington Avenue, it
climbed the Inclenberg grade (starting at about Thirty-
second Street), and after passing Mr. Murray's driveway and formal gardens jogged east toward Turtle Bay
and then swung back gradually toward the middle of the
island. The distance from the Kip's Bay shore to the
Post Road on Inclenberg was not more than six hundred
yards, and that was one of the reasons Howe had picked
it as a second-choice landing site; if all went well, the
leading British troops should have control of the vital
artery in short order.

At about ten o'clock Douglas and his men began to
suspect that they were in for worse than just naval gunfire. There was a flotilla of landing barges—eighty-four
of them—on the far shore of the East River, at the

mouth of Newtown Creek, which separates Brooklyn
from Queens. Howe's light infantrymen, who led the way
in an assault landing, began boarding the boats. As soon
as each boat had its complement of soldiers aboard, it
was rowed to a rendezvous point in the lee of a group
of transports anchored close to the Brooklyn shore. Not
long after the last of the landing boats had joined the
others, the oarsmen began pulling for Kip's Bay.

As the boats advanced, the incoming tide caught the
line and bent it into a crescent, carrying the procession
upstream. The British soldiers in the boats were standing in ranks with their muskets, bayonets fixed, on their
shoulders. In their brilliant scarlet and white they made
a splendid, frightening sight.

It was all that Douglas' hungry men needed to complete their demoralization, but before they could do
anything about it the sailors on the ships right in front
of them jumped into action; the start of the assault
boats across the river was the signal for the five frigates
in the Bay to let go the broadsides the Americans had
been awaiting since dawn.

Shortly before eleven o'clock the entire line fired at
once, with a thunderous crack of powder, and eighty-
six cannon balls sizzled ashore. Dust, smoke, and clumps
of sod filled the air. Martin, the militiaman who had
been trying to decipher the papers in the shed, was
scared out of his wits; he made "a frog's leap," as he
later described it, for what momentarily seemed the
safety of his shallow trench. He cowered there, with
his fellow soldiers, making himself as small as he could,

but feeling certain that despite his best efforts the next
cannon ball would surely hit him.

After the initial, stunning blast, the cannon continued
to fire as fast as they could be loaded. Douglas' men
felt that the British gunners could look—and shoot—
right down into the American trenches from above. The
ships' cannon were slightly above the level of the shore,
and besides the main batteries there were a number of
smaller pieces, called swivels—a cross between a big
musket and a cannon—mounted in the rigging and therefore firing from an even higher elevation. The British
could see the Americans easily enough, but most of their
artillery did not depress below the horizontal; nearly
all their shots were too high and went whistling over the
trenches, over the heads of Douglas' men, and into the
meadow behind. The cloud of dust and smoke, which
one eyewitness, Benjamin Trumbull, a chaplain, described as "burying" the Americans, may have helped
spoil the gunners' aim, but it added to the shore defenders' feelings of terror and helplessness; they had no
way of retaliating against the bombardment and, without being able to see how far the assault boats had pro-
gressed, they realized that the light infantry was headed
right for their section of the river line.

Almost no one was actually hit by the British bombardment, but the situation was too much for the Connecticut recruits. The men in the regiment on Douglas'
left, who were getting most of the ships' attention,
broke and ran. They abandoned their trenches and fled
for cover into the woods at the edge of the meadow.

The panic, starting in the weakest regiment, spread rapidly down the line from north to south. By the time the
leading British assault boats drew even with the line of
warships—at which moment the bombardment ended—
only a few men, Colonel Douglas included, remained in
position, and they were on the far right where the shelling had been much the lightest.

The booming of the cannon, which had continued for
most of an hour, was heard all over the island. Washington heard it in Harlem, and realizing that something
unexpected was happening, he and his command party
started riding at full speed in the direction of the ominous sounds. General Putnam, in the city, heard it and at
once ordered General John Fellows' brigade and three
regiments of General Samuel H. Parsons' brigade to
leave the fortifications they had been manning at Corlear's Hook (the southernmost point of land on the
East River, and in recent years a small park beside the
Franklin D. Roosevelt Drive, a couple of blocks south
of the Williamsburg Bridge) and march north to reinforce wherever reinforcing was needed.

The troops nearest Douglas' section of the river line
—General James Wadsworth's brigade, which was in
the vicinity of what is now Twenty-third Street, and
General John Scott's brigade, on the shore behind the
Peter Stuyvesant house, near the foot of Sixteenth Street
—not only heard the gunfire but saw the oncoming
swarm of landing craft. According to the general scheme
of the defense, Wadsworth's five regiments of Connect-

icut levies and Scott's four regiments of New Yorkers
should have hurried to Douglas' assistance as soon as
it was clear that the landing was aimed at Kip's Bay.
They failed to do so. A good many of the men were as
panicky as Douglas' soldiers; others believed a false
rumor that swept along the river bank to the effect that
a retreat had been ordered. In a very short time the
woods and the roads were filled with men in motion,
hurrying in every direction. Men were running away
from their commanders and men were looking for a
commander to report to. Some units were scattered and
out of control, and others were in good order and marching purposefully—toward what no one exactly knew.

Almost immediately the Post Road was a mad snarl of
marchers and horsemen moving in both directions; the
traffic heading north was considerably heavier than the
southbound, but everybody was pushing to get somewhere, or shouting orders, or passing along the latest
alarm. For all the bustle of activity, hardly anyone
moved in the direction of the meadow behind Kip's Bay.
By design or otherwise, the soldiers marching north,
when they reached the Twenty-third Street fork, all
took the Bloomingdale Road to the left instead of the
Post Road to the right—and it was on the Post Road
that reinforcements were needed. No organized group
of men larger than squad size arrived on the battlefield
before Colonel Douglas and the handful of soldiers who
had stuck with him decided that their position was hopeless, and retreated from the field. As soon as the first
British infantrymen scrambled up the rocks, near the

Kip farmhouse, the area belonged to General Howe. He
had won it by default.

There were about four thousand men in the British
assault force, which was under the command of Lieutenant General Sir Henry Clinton, the son of a former
Royal Governor of New York. He had three battalions
of light infantry, four battalions of British grenadiers,
three battalions of Hessian grenadiers and jaegers, and
a brigade of British guards. They constituted a kind
of élite advance section of the British army, and their
assignment was to establish a beachhead, hold it against
possible counterattack, and guard its perimeter while
the main body of Howe's forces, an additional nine thousand men, was being ferried across the river on a flat-
boat shuttle system.

Clinton's first division, as the advance third of the
army was called, carried out their mission with clock-
work competence. Brigadier General Alexander Leslie's
light infantry landed first and moved to the right,
through the north side of the meadow; on their heels
came the British grenadiers, commanded by Lieutenant
General Earl Cornwallis and Major General John
Vaughan, whose objective was the high ground, Inclenberg, straight ahead. And Colonel Carl von Donop's
Hessians (the grenadiers in blue coats and the jaegers
in green) completed the fanning out by turning toward
the south, heading for the woods and orchards on the
Watts property. Since there was no resistance beyond
an occasional flurry of musket shots from the few Americans who had not run all the way away, there was little

to interfere with the parade-ground precision of the normal British drill. Clinton's troops marched closed up and with their lines dressed, keeping in cadence with their beating drums. Their formality and their gaudy uniforms (with the trousers, straps, and belts freshly whitened with pipe-clay paste) may have seemed almost comic; but as old-timers in the American army, especially the veterans of the French and Indian War, knew very well, the brilliant appearance of the British soldiers— maintained at the cost of constant effort and endless cleaning, polishing, and daubing with clay—was a sign of their remarkable discipline.

They marched to their assigned positions on the limits of the semicircular beachhead, and only one minor skirmish interrupted the otherwise effortless maneuver. On the British left, in one of the Watts orchards, a handful of Americans stood for a little while in the way of the Hessians' progress. Von Donop's men had a style of fighting all their own. In an advance, like this one, the jaegers, in exception to the general close-order style of march, moved ahead of the grenadiers in an open, irregular fashion, running from point to point and ducking behind trees and boulders. In this they were rather like the Americans, who had learned to fight Indians that way on the frontier, and had not yet as an army adopted a strict, standardized system of infantry drill, although they needed one badly. But there was a marked difference between leading the way for grenadiers— which is what the jaegers did—and fighting Indian style for lack of a superior technique; the fighting on Long

Island had shown the limitations of the free-and-easy
American method, for inexperienced soldiers without
training in a drill have to learn to make a stand on a
formal, open battlefield. Not many of Washington's men
had had combat experience of any kind, and, like frontiersmen (and Indians), some of them had shown a
tendency to give up their ground and melt away into the
woods when the going got rough. Many of von Donop's
jaegers had been professional hunters or game wardens
in Germany, carried rifles instead of smooth-bore muskets, and were consequently regarded, with some justifi-
cation, as sharpshooters; they took aim at particular
targets instead of merely pointing in the general direction of the enemy and firing as a group in volleys—which
was all that musketmen could do. The jaegers' rifles
were reasonably accurate at distances of up to one hundred yards.

But von Donop's real power was in the Hessian grenadiers. They followed along behind the screen of jaegers
and they marched in formal column; and whenever the
jaegers encountered any opposition that they couldn't
easily drive out of the way, the grenadiers were expected
to steam-roller their column through it. The grenadiers
carried muskets with attached bayonets; and their bayonets, rather than powder and shot, were their basic
weapons, as they were for the British army as a whole.
If anyone dared stand in their path, the grenadiers
formed a firing line, let go a volley or two with their
muskets—as much for psychological effect as in the ex-
pectation of hitting anybody—and then lowered their

bayonets for a running charge. The mere thought of Hessian bayonets was enough to give American soldiers nightmares, partly because they didn't have many themselves and hadn't been taught to use those they had. And partly because every American, soldier and civilian alike, had heard terrifying tales about the brutality with which the Hessians were supposed to employ the weapon. There was no clear-cut proof that a bayonet in Hessian hands was any more horrible than, say, a British bayonet; but there was also no doubt that both British and Hessian soldiers, in the fury of a bayonet charge, were capable of savagery—and that they sometimes stabbed Americans who had given up and were trying to surrender. (For the truth is that soldiers trained to the point of efficiency that makes a bayonet charge possible cannot be expected to charge in a considerate manner.)

Within about an hour after they had landed, von Donop's battalions had secured the south and southwestern boundaries of the beachhead and had cleared away all the Americans in the area. They had killed between thirty and forty Americans and had taken sixty prisoners, including some who had not meant to engage the Hessians but had merely wandered into their way in the confusion. By midday or a little later Clinton had accomplished his immediate purpose: he was in good control of the Kip's Bay assembly point. He was in possession of Inclenberg; he held the Post Road from below Sunfish Pond to north of the Murray mansion's driveway; and his troops were spread out all around the edge of the large semicircle ready to stand off any attempt by the

Americans to recapture the ground they had lost. All this had been achieved with only one important British casualty. That was General Vaughan. As he marched across the meadow and up Inclenberg toward the Murray house, he had been nicked by a musket ball.

III

GENERAL WASHINGTON and his aides approached
the scene just as Clinton's men had finished taking
the beachhead. Brigadier General Thomas Mifflin, whose
men were in reserve on Harlem Heights, was with them.
The party galloped down the Post Road, past the Turtle
Bay turnoff, until they reached a point somewhere between the present Lexington and Third avenues in the
lower Forties, not far north of Inclenberg. There they
ran into a rabble of men from Douglas' and Wadsworth's brigades who were in full flight, hurrying north
as fast as they could go. There was no noise of skirmishing behind them, and Washington saw no sign of enemy
troops—although, as a matter of fact, Leslie's light infantrymen were only a few hundred yards farther on
down the highway. The British were not pursuing the
fugitives, because they had orders, which they were
obeying, to stop when they reached the beachhead's
boundary.

The sight of his soldiers running away—and apparently running from nothing at all—shocked Washing-

45

ton. He and his aides, with General Mifflin's help, tried
to stop the stampede. Waving their swords and pistols
and shouting curses, the mounted men did their best to
ride herd on the panic-stricken soldiers and block their
flight, but it was impossible. The retreat had gained too
much momentum, and when the officers put themselves
in its way, the militiamen abandoned the road and took
off through the fields and woods. The tide swept right
past and around the Commander-in-Chief and on north,
heading in the general direction of Harlem Heights.

Meanwhile Fellows' and Parsons' brigades, which
had come up from Corlear's Hook, had arrived on the
western and southwestern side of Clinton's beachhead,
and in reasonably good order. They had marched north
up the Post Road in column of regiments and, like almost everyone else, they had gone left at the Twenty-
third Street fork and onto the Bloomingdale Road, thus
veering well to the west of where they were badly
needed. Considering the Post Road's congestion, and
the helter-skelter of hurrying to and fro, the two brigades' company officers had done exceedingly well to
keep control at all and to maintain their units' positions
in the line of march. Added to their other difficulties, the
day by now had become exceedingly hot, and the dust
kicked up by all the activity hung over the scene in a
vast cloud.

Not far north of Inclenberg there was a minor crossroad connecting the Bloomingdale and Post roads. It
was bordered by stone walls and, behind them, cultivated fields. If it were still there, it would cross over

from Broadway at about Forty-third Street to Lexington Avenue and Forty-first Street, passing Bryant Park and the north end of the Public Library on approximately the Forty-second Street line. The leading regiment of Fellows' brigade, at the head of the long column of reinforcements, turned right off the Bloomingdale Road and into this crossroad and came to a halt. Parsons' outfit, behind Fellows', halted, too, with its head on the Bloomingdale Road.

At nearly the same time, Washington's party, fresh from its failure to stop the runaways, rode into the crossroad from its other end, at the Post Road. Washington took a position just south of the crossroad and near its middle, close to what is now Forty-second Street and Fifth Avenue, and began to piece together a picture of the situation.

While his aides rode off, hunting for commanders and trying to pick up scraps of reliable information, Washington's subordinates rode up to him to report and receive new orders. Putnam, who had ridden all the way from the city, discussed the developments with the Commander-in-Chief. So did Major General Joseph Spencer, who, as a temporary substitute for General Greene, was in command of all the brigades that had been guarding the middle stretches of the East River shore—the so-called middle division that had just disgraced itself. And so did General Fellows and General Parsons, whose brigades, while they had made no contact with the enemy, were at least intact—present, accounted for, and apparently ready to put up some sort of fight against the invaders.

It was not too late to make a stand, Washington believed. And the crossroad, with its fences, offered an obvious place to try to form a battle line. Washington ordered Fellows and Parsons to march their brigades forward as they were headed, and to bring both outfits into the crossroad. There they could at least hope to maintain a position and to keep General Howe from extending his beachhead any farther to the north.

This seemed a reasonable tactic. But when Fellows and Parsons passed the word along, and their junior officers tried to get the halted column to march again, they lost the control they had maintained all the way from Corlear's Hook. All at once the spell of military authority disintegrated; and as men saw other men disregarding commands, the long formation came apart. Within a few minutes soldiers were running aimlessly here and there, or dashing out of ranks and running off across country, and what had been a potent holding force degenerated into a formless, unmanageable mob. As soon as the line of marchers broke up, the individual soldiers got hopelessly mixed up with stragglers from Douglas', Wadsworth's, and Scott's brigades, some of whom were still milling aimlessly about.

Washington, angered by his troops' inability to execute a simple forward march, broke the rule that a general should never attempt to do a lieutenant's work. He made the same mistake, and with no better results, that he had made only a short time earlier; he tried, personally, to put some backbone into his demoralized men. Washington and his aides rode up and down the cross-road, trying desperately to organize the men already on it into a line of resistance.

"Take the wall! Take the cornfield!" Washington shouted, pointing to the positions along the road.

A few soldiers obediently got into place behind the fences, but most of them stayed only until the Commander's party had ridden past and then joined the majority, running north; and a great many more, as the mounting confusion fed upon itself, ignored the commands completely. At the height of the fiasco some British soldiers came into sight on the crest of Inclenberg, not more than a quarter of a mile to the south. They were an advance detachment of about seventy men, but they were the first of the enemy that Fellows' and Parsons' troops had seen that day, and their appearance completed the rout that panic and rumor had started.

When Washington realized that the situation was hopeless—that his soldiers were incapable of standing and trying to make a fight for the crossroad—he lost the last vestiges of his self-control. He tore off his hat and dashed it to the ground. Cursing violently, he roared that his men were not men at all but scum, and that the war itself was impossible with cowards for soldiers. In his fury he slashed at both officers and men with his riding crop, trying to beat courage into them. But the General's frenzy, formidable as it was, accomplished nothing. His troops continued to break away, leaving Washington and his aides practically alone on the crossroad,

amid a litter of equipment—muskets, powder horns,
knapsacks, hats, coats—that had been thrown aside to
make running easier.

Presently someone in the General's party noticed that
the enemy detachment was advancing cautiously in their
direction. Since no one in the group had any weapon
more effective than a sword or a pistol, there was some
real danger that the Commander-in-Chief, if he stayed
too long, might be shot or even taken prisoner. But
though it was obvious that the time had come to flee,
Washington unaccountably failed to spur his horse. He
simply sat dejectedly in his saddle, with his head bowed,
as if he had lost track of what had happened or where
he was. He seemed utterly exhausted by the intensity of
his tantrum, and in a kind of daze. His aides weren't
sure what to do. They waited as long as they dared, until
the leading British soldiers were almost within musket
range, and then, finally, one of them took the bridle of
the General's horse and led him away.

With the Post Road cut and the Bloomingdale Road
threatened—and with nothing to prevent Howe from
enlarging the size of the beachhead as soon as he was
ready to do so—all the American soldiers south of the
landing area were in danger of being cut off. There was
no telling how soon Howe's troops might be ordered to
march west to the Hudson, sealing off everything below,
say, the Thirty-fourth Street line. No one was more
keenly aware of this than General Putnam, who after
his conference with Washington had ridden back down

the Post Road toward the city in order to halt the evacuation work and try to hurry his troops out of the trap
before it closed. Fellows' and Parsons' brigades, although they were in the process of disgracing themselves, were no problem; most of them were safely north
of the potential cutoff line and could be expected, whatever happened, to make their way to the Heights and
rejoin the main body of the army. But more than half
the men in Putnam's force—Colonel Gold Silliman's
brigade, Colonel Henry Knox's artillery, and a number
of other units that were part of the rear guard—were in
or below the city's fortifications. There were close to
three thousand of them in all, and their chances of escaping seemed slim.

Putnam was fifty-eight years old, short and stocky,
round-faced and optimistic. He had been poor as a boy
and had not had much formal education. As a general
officer he knew little about such matters as logistics,
strategy, and staff administration. But on the field he
was a fine troop leader; he had an extraordinary amount
of energy and enterprise, and above all he was famous
among his men for what one of his adjutants called "deliberate fortitude." Almost everybody called him "Old
Put" (behind his back, of course), and it was axio-
matic that, at the sound of shooting, Old Put would
naturally wheel his horse and head in the direction of
the fray. His home was in Pomfret, Connecticut, where
he had established himself as a fairly well-to-do farmer
before the beginning of the French and Indian War, and
it was characteristic of him that, as a captain, he had

led the first Connecticut company sent out in 1755. He was admired as a hero by most of his soldiers, and countless incredible anecdotes (some entirely true) were told about his military adventures: how Old Put had escaped being burned at the stake by Indians; Old Put's shipwreck off the coast of Cuba; Old Put's wild ride, at full gallop down a precipitous flight of rocky steps, to keep from being captured by the British; and others in the same vein.

The idea Putnam had in mind now was a bold one: he meant to try to rush his troops up the west side of the island, keeping as far as possible from the beachhead, in the hope that they might slip past Clinton's men. The rear guard was scattered over a rather large area, and getting word to all the units was no small task.

Putnam was fortunate in having as one of his aides Major Aaron Burr, who knew the terrain well. Burr was twenty years old and had been one of Washington's aides for a week or so earlier in the year. But the young major, who had served with distinction at Quebec, had been unhappy about the endless paper work at the Commander-in-Chief's headquarters, and had resigned in disgust. He felt he was at his best in just the kind of role the emergency now demanded, dashing about on his horse, rounding up stragglers, and directing them to the main column of escaping marchers.

Putnam and his subordinates ordered all the troops in New York to forget their evacuation work and to prepare as quickly as possible for the twelve-mile forced march to Harlem Heights. It meant abandoning all

kinds of supplies the army needed badly, tents and ord-
nance in particular. Colonel Knox had to leave behind
a total of sixty-seven guns and more than thirteen thousand rounds of artillery ammunition. Most of the guns
were old, and a good many of them had defective bar-
rels or were worn to the point of being dangerous to fire;
still, their loss was a most serious matter. They were not
in much worse shape than many of the cannon Knox had
managed to move north, and in numbers the sixty-seven
pieces represented more than half of all the artillery
Washington's army possessed.

Although the men in the city had been aware for several days that they were to leave before long, they were
almost as unprepared for the sudden march order as if
it had been a complete surprise. The sound of the Kip's
Bay bombardment, and the rumors brought by those
men who had run south from their positions along the
river instead of north, had added confusion; it was possible, in view of the landing, that they were now expected
to man the fortifications line and attempt to hold the
British north of New York, in spite of the older plan of
retreat. Until they got definite word about Putnam's
daring scheme, unit commanders could hardly know
what to do. A few heard about the march late, and some
were not notified at all, but what was most remarkable
was the efficiency with which Putnam's staff worked;
they got nearly everybody rounded up and moving out
in an extraordinarily short time. The head of the column
of some three thousand marchers left New York at four
in the afternoon, following the Greenwich Road, close

to the Hudson, toward Greenwich, a district of hand-some farms and country houses that included most of what is now called Chelsea as well as the present Greenwich Village area.

Captain Sebastian Bauman, commanding one of Knox's artillery companies, was one of the officers who failed to fall in with Putnam's main body of marchers, and his experiences with his unit were typical of the difficulties that Putnam, for the most part, solved. Bauman's company had been on the Grand Battery, the southernmost tip of the island, when the Kip's Bay attack started. He had two howitzers and standing orders that he was to bring them out of the city—if he left it—at the risk of his life. Shortly after ten o'clock, when the bombardment was rumbling uptown, Bauman was ordered to move his men, or force his way if necessary, into Bunker's Hill, a sod redoubt, one of the main strong points in the city's line of fortifications, on a hill near the present intersection of Grand and Centre streets. He dutifully marched through New York with his drums and fifes playing and his howitzers in tow. The field-pieces were the only guns the company had, for not a single man in it was equipped with a musket. Bauman had a feeling that the town had been deserted. En route to the fort, he saw only half a dozen other soldiers.

There were troops at Bunker's Hill, however, including about twenty-five men with muskets; and for several hours Bauman believed the prevailing rumors in the strongpoint: that the British had extended their line from Kip's Bay almost to the Hudson; that his company

and the others in the fortifications had been entirely cut
off, but, as the fate of war had it, they were to hold the
line as long as possible without any real hope of with-
standing a British siege.

When Bauman got Putnam's march order at about
four o'clock, he did not understand that his company was
to join several thousand marchers; he thought that his
little group by itself was expected to fight its own way
through Howe's combined divisions to King's Bridge—
an even more preposterous thought than the prospect of
standing off the British with twenty-five muskets and
two howitzers.

Nevertheless Bauman started his company with some
of the musketeers—a total of about eighty men—on the
way. He left Bunker's Hill, marched west and then
north a short distance, and although with reasonable
luck he should have bumped into at least the tail end of
Putnam's column, he failed to do so. The sight of two
British warships lying close to the shore brought Bauman to a halt; if they fired at him, he thought, Howe's
whole army would descend upon him in no time. He hid
his men and his two howitzers in a small, deserted redoubt and sent two scouts, a corporal and a gunner, on
reconnaissance, hoping to discover just where the enemy's troops were. It got dark. The scouts did not return, and Bauman decided it would be safer to try to
return to Bunker's Hill under cover of darkness, and
spend the rest of the night in that comparatively well-
built structure. But as the company moved from the redoubt, headed for the fort and keeping as quiet as it

possibly could, someone spotted an abandoned sailboat, with its sails up, high and dry on the beach. The sailboat offered a chance of getting away and making for Paulus Hook (Jersey City) across the Hudson.

With considerable effort Bauman's men pushed the sailboat off the beach and into the water before they discovered, to the Captain's dismay, that it was too small to carry the howitzers. Not realizing that more than half the other guns had already been abandoned, and knowing only that his two were supposed to be as valuable as his life, Captain Bauman apparently never considered leaving the artillery behind. Instead he sent the sailboat, loaded with men, to Paulus Hook and ordered a crew to return, if possible, with a bigger boat. In addition—just to make sure—he sent a corporal down the river bank toward the city on the off chance that he might be able to turn up something, if only a raft, large enough to transport the two fieldpieces.

Meanwhile Bauman, with the balance of his men, settled down on the shore near the guns to wait. The time passed frightfully slowly, and the men expected that at any moment Howe's army would discover them. After a long time the corporal came back; he had been unable to find anything useful. Finally, at close to midnight, the cannoneers from Paulus Hook showed up. They had found another boat. It was large enough for the guns, for Captain Bauman and the rest of the men in the company. And off they went, to their own great relief, to the safety of the New Jersey shore.

Putnam's column was a long one. Its advance guard
reached the William Bayard and Oliver De Lancey
estates, near what is now Twenty-third Street, before
the tail of the formation had passed the present Cham-
bers Street. It was difficult to keep the infantry marching fast, although Putnam assumed that speed was the
only thing that could save them. While the skies were
clouding, the afternoon was still oppressively hot, and
the soldiers' canteens were soon empty. But spurring on
a body of marching men was exactly the kind of job
Putnam could handle to perfection. He raced up and
down the column, his horse wild-eyed and flecked with
foam, shouting encouragement and urging his men
to maintain the pace. Flank guards struggled over the
rough terrain, mostly farmlands, a few hundred yards
to the east of the main body, on the watch for signs of
British activity. Putnam would not have been surprised
if the column had encountered a line of British troops,
or at least an enemy road block, at any point north of
Greenwich. Beyond there, as far as to what is now
Columbus Circle, the route of march followed farm
lanes and footpaths along a line that approximated the
present course of Eighth Avenue. It joined the Bloomingdale Road at about the present Fifty-ninth Street,
and followed it the rest of the way up the West Side.
It was possible that Putnam's men could have forced
their way through a British attempt to stop them, but
the question did not come up; to the Americans' surprise
they marched past the critical point—directly opposite

Kip's Bay—without finding a single British soldier in
their way.

The fact of the matter was that Howe had not sent
any troops from the initial beachhead across to the West
Side or to the Hudson. There was no river-to-river British line across Thirty-fourth Street, nor did Howe intend to establish one there. Clinton's leading division
was right where it had been since shortly past the noon
hour—on and around Inclenberg, holding the perimeter
of the beachhead and waiting for the landing-craft ferry
system to finish the tedious job of bringing in the nine
thousand men in the second division—five brigades and
two regiments of British regulars, a brigade of Hessians,
and the artillery—across the East River. That was according to plan, and the plan was being executed perfectly.

If Howe's concept of the proper management of an
amphibious assault had been less sound, he might have
saved himself much subsequent criticism. He believed
that the landing force ought to build up as much strength
as possible within its initial beachhead before it attempted to move ahead toward the next objectives, and,
in the years since, no one has been able to improve upon
that as a basic tactical rule in the conduct of a water-
borne infantry landing. Howe's plan gave the Americans credit for being able to put up some sort of opposition to his assault; it assumed that at first Clinton's
troops might have their hands full with the problems of
taking the beachhead. Afterwards, in view of the
Americans' utter, though scarcely predictable, collapse,

Howe's impeccable tactics seemed excessively cautious. He had won on the strength of his preliminary naval bombardment alone but had missed his chance to cut off Putnam's three thousand men, nearly one fifth of Washington's total number of effectives; and Englishmen and Americans alike never let him forget it.

Howe was forty-seven years old. He was dark-complexioned, tall, and his bearing was soldierly despite his pronounced paunch—a tribute to his great fondness for food and drink. He was a professional soldier, above everything else, who had been working at his occupation since he was seventeen. He had had considerable military experience on the European continent, and in America during the French and Indian War, and he had shown unusual courage on the battlefield. Like his older brother, Richard, Admiral Lord Howe, commanding the British fleet at New York, Sir William was a man of few words. He kept his own counsel so carefully and talked about himself so little that even the staff officers closest to him were not sure just what his private attitudes were; but there was no question that tactical planning was first among his professional abilities. His careful, detailed battle orders could seldom be faulted.

Yet Howe was charged with being more interested in his technical victories, battle by battle, than in exploiting the successes he won. He repeatedly outmaneuvered Washington, as he had at Kip's Bay, and scored easily, like an expert boxer amassing points, but failed to come even close to victory by a knockout. And later on, after a series of less-than-decisive wins, King George III and

the Tory Party in England began to interpret Howe's
military record as an expression of his character, both
political and moral, and took a dim view of the con-
sistency they saw. It was then that much was made of
Howe's prewar record as a Whig: as a candidate for
Parliament from Nottingham in 1774 he had said he
was so much opposed to using force against the Colonies
that, if offered an American command, he would refuse
it. (He excused himself for having broken his word on
the grounds that he had been given no real choice; that
the King had not offered him a post but had ordered
him to report to Lieutenant General Thomas Gage at
Boston, and then had put him in Gage's place in October, 1775.) He was accused of harboring pro-American
sentiments, and indeed he hoped even after the Battle
of Long Island that some basis for a negotiated peace
could still be found.

On a personal level Howe was criticized for eating,
drinking, and gambling to excess, and for spending too
much time with the handsome, blonde Mrs. Joshua Loring, whom he had met in Boston and then taken with
him to Halifax and New York. (Mr. Loring, who accompanied them, seemed satisfied, as his part of the
arrangement, with an appointment as Howe's Commis-
sary for Prisoners.) And these indulgences, according
to the General's detractors, robbed him of whatever will
to win he may have had in the first place.

Putnam's column escaped, but there was not the
slightest evidence that Howe was doing anything less
than his best on the afternoon of September 15th. It took

about three hours—from two o'clock until nearly five—
to land the second division and complete the build-up.
During that interval the British soldiers picked up a
few more American prisoners, and at Mrs. Robert Murray's invitation Howe, with Clinton, Cornwallis, and a
few of the other officers, had cakes and Madeira sherry
in the Murray house. There is a romantic legend that
despite her husband's sympathy for the British cause
Mrs. Murray was an ardent patriot, and that she gave
the party in order to delay Howe and give Putnam's
men time to get away to Harlem Heights; but it loses
most of its luster on two accounts. Mrs. Murray, however she felt about the American cause, could not have
known that Putnam was trying to escape—he might
have decided, after his conference with Washington, to
defend the city's fortifications to the last man. And,
secondly, the British officers were not delayed. Howe's
written battle order, while it said nothing about refresh-
ments, did specify a wait on Inclenberg. Just as soon as
his whole force was ashore, Howe went ahead with the
next phase of his attack, entirely in accordance with his
plan.

At five o'clock a Hessian brigade moved south from
the beachhead toward the city, marching down the Post
Road and occupying the houses, barns, and buildings
along the way. And to complete the seizure of New
York itself a detachment from the British fleet landed
in small boats on the tip of the island and took possession of the abandoned town. At the same time the main
body of Howe's men, with the light infantry in the lead,

marched north on the Post Road heading for McGown's
Pass at about what is now 106th Street, a few hundred
yards west of Fifth Avenue, inside Central Park.

The British were following a route that a great many
of the runaways had taken, but by this time Washington
had posted Colonel William Smallwood's Marylanders
in the enemy's path. This outfit had taken up a position
at about what is now Ninety-sixth Street and Fifth Avenue, and its orders were to delay the British if they
should move in that direction, and so give Sargent's men
from the battery at Horn's Hook and the other units on
the East River in the vicinity of Harlem as much time
as possible to complete their withdrawal to the Heights.

Although he was half a mile south of it, Smallwood
was actually guarding McGown's Pass. That defile, where
the Post Road ran between two steep hills and then
zigzagged down a sharp grade from comparatively high
ground to the Harlem Plains, was the best place on the
highway for a small force to make a stand against an
advancing army. (Central Park's East Drive now descends in much the same way as the Post Road did then;
it sweeps in an S-curve down to the level of the Harlem
Meer, the small lake in the northeast corner of the Park.
A short distance east of where the Drive starts to curve,
on top of one of the McGown's Pass hills, there is a small,
rectangular lookout with a few benches, an 1812-vintage
cannon, and a memorial plaque.) Smallwood was prepared to fall back to the Pass if necessary, but he intended to yield the ground as slowly as possible. And
the ground between his initial position and the defile,

like most of the island's terrain, favored a defensive holding action; the ground was hilly, with many out-croppings of rock and a profusion of small valleys and draws. Its ruggedness, combined with the trees and un-derbrush that covered all the landscape except those fields that were under cultivation, would persuade the British to keep to the roads, as far as practicable, in order to maintain their formations. At the same time the ground offered good cover and concealment for the Americans, who, with their irregular tactics, could make the most of them.

As the British column came on, marching smartly across the upper East Side, Putnam's troops were mak-ing good time on the Bloomingdale Road. It was an ab-surd situation: two large bodies of soldiers moving in the same direction on very nearly parallel routes, not a great deal farther apart than the width of Central Park, and with both commanders completely unaware of what the other was doing.

Leslie's light infantry, the spearhead of the British advance, approached Smallwood's position, and the Marylanders held their ground—the first time all day that an American outfit had been able to offer the Brit-ish any kind of organized resistance. The regiment's spirit, in contrast to that of so many other units in Washington's army, was high. It had existed as part of the militia before the war, and it was largely made up of the sons of leading Baltimore and Annapolis families. Nearly all of the Marylanders wore brown hunting shirts in the style of frontiersmen, a uniform that Washington approved highly and wished there were more of, for it was not only comfortable and practical but it implied that its wearer was a good shot. Consequently the British respected hunting shirts in the same spirit with which Americans looked seriously at the uniforms of the Hessian grenadiers.

There was a short, sharp exchange of musket fire between Smallwood's and Leslie's men, and then the British, finding that the Americans were prepared to make a fight for the Post Road, turned west onto a side road called the New Bloomingdale Crossroad that ran across the island and into the Bloomingdale Road at a point not far south of Striker's Bay. The intersection was at about what is now Ninety-first Street and Broadway.

Smallwood's stand had unexpectedly turned Howe's column in the direction of Putnam's marching troops. As the British proceeded crosstown, a rain squall suddenly ended the stifling heat and settled the dust that had bothered both armies all during the afternoon. The leading British company approached the Bloomingdale Road, but too late to block Putnam's way. By the time Leslie's men reached the intersection, all of the Americans except the last regiment in the line of marchers— the 2nd Connecticut Militia—had safely passed it. There was a brief skirmish on the spot, within sight of Charles Apthorpe's large white country house. (Mr. Apthorpe, a Tory, had fled Manhattan in July.) The Connecticut men held off the British for a time while the main column plodded on north. Then the rear guard retreated, following the others in the direction of the Heights.

Only one man had fallen in the brief action: the regimental commander, Lieutenant Colonel Jabez Thompson.

That ended the day's fighting. Smallwood's Marylanders retreated, after their short but effective engagement, according to prearrangement. They left McGown's Pass open to the British, who took the position but did not venture beyond it; they made it one of the pivotal points in the line they established for the night. Putnam's men reached Harlem Heights, although it was dark before the 2nd Connecticut reported in. The forced march had exhausted a good many of the soldiers, and their morale was low, but most of them considered themselves lucky to be there. And as the two armies settled down in their respective camps, everything south of the line from Striker's Bay through McGown's Pass to Horn's Hook belonged to General Howe. It had all gone just as the British commander had planned, and the cost of southern Manhattan—a mere handful of British casualties—had been even less than he had anticipated.

IV

THE Harlem Heights camp was a gloomy place the
night of the fifteenth. Except for the technical advantage that Washington's army was now pulled together into a single body, there was nothing to be cheer-
ful about. Even though the loss of the city had been
determined earlier, and Washington and his council of
military advisers had done their best to discount the retreat in their own minds, the actual process of being
driven from New York was a blow to the morale of
both officers and men. But that was almost trifling compared to the depressing effect of the thought that General Spencer's middle-division brigades had come apart
at the seams, and that Fellows' and Parsons' had done
little better. The men in the ranks could only feel
ashamed of themselves. With few exceptions they were
unable to raise their spirits by boasting about anything
they had done, and the stories they told were lugubrious.
(One rumor, for instance, concerned a soldier who had
run so fast in the noonday heat that when he stopped
for a drink at a spring the shock of the cold water killed

66

him.) The men who had been involved at Kip's Bay and on Inclenberg were gloomiest of all; for the most part they were silent and sullen, hating themselves and their officers in about equal measure.

To make things worse, it had turned cold after the rain. The rations situation had not improved; a man was lucky to get anything at all to eat. There were by no means enough tents to accommodate everybody—the tent shortage was worse than ever on account of the canvas that had been abandoned with the other supplies in New York, and the number of soldiers on the Heights was nearly double what it had been the night before. Private Martin's regiment, in Douglas' brigade, had only one tent for the entire outfit. Most of the other units were not quite so badly off, but many soldiers had no shelter at all, and had to sleep in their damp clothes on the wet ground right out in the open.

Washington's troops had suffered fifty or sixty casualties during the day, and about twenty officers and three hundred men had been taken prisoner. A number of others—like Bauman's company, for instance—were missing, at least temporarily. (The reckoning of the American losses was only approximate, for the army had yet to establish a precise system of keeping track of casualties.) Considering how little real fighting had taken place, the day's toll was discouragingly high. But at headquarters at the Morris house, to which Washington had returned in midafternoon, the question of losses— like all the other results of what had happened on the fifteenth—was far less important than the problems the sixteenth raised. There was no time for post-mortems; for all the General knew, Howe might be planning to attack the Heights the first thing in the morning, and it was imperative that the Americans prepare for such an attack at once.

One good example of something that would have required immediate attention, under less pressing circumstances, was the question of Colonel Robert Tyler, the commander of one of the regiments in Parsons' brigade. Washington was convinced—although it later turned out that the General was wrong—that Tyler had acted with cowardice during the attempt to form a line on the crossroad behind Inclenberg. But even a matter of that seriousness had to be put aside temporarily. (Twelve days later Tyler was arrested. A court of inquiry, some time afterward, found nothing to support Washington's interpretation of the Colonel's actions—and, in fact, a number of eyewitnesses testified that the Colonel had done his best to lead his men into fighting position.)

By modern standards, army headquarters was tiny. Washington's entire force, to be sure, was only slightly larger (at least in number of effectives) than one modern army division; but the Commander-in-Chief had little of the expert staff help that a division commander now gets as a matter of routine, and he had an enormous amount of work to do. Since there was no mechanical means of communication, just the number of man-hours spent on issuing orders was formidable. Most of the orders had to be written in longhand, edited, copied by hand,

and then delivered by messenger. Verbal orders were not much less trouble. Subordinate commanders could be assembled for a conference and told what to do, but the process was slow and often, in the midst of an action, a practical impossibility. The alternative was to send word by an aide who was understood to speak with the General's authority. In short, headquarters was as much a message center as a command post, and Washington himself, writing out rough drafts of orders, letters and reports, was compelled to spend hours of every normal day trying to keep up with the mass of paper work. He had only eleven assistants, and they were invariably far behind.

Besides his three aides—George Baylor, Samuel Webb, and Richard Cary—Washington had assigned himself an acting aide, Tench Tilghman, and two special aides, George Lewis and Caleb Gibbs, who were supposed, technically, to belong to the headquarters guard. He had a military secretary, Robert Hanson Harrison, and Harrison in turn had two assistants: Alexander Contee Hanson and William Grayson. The other two members of Washington's family, both former aides who had been promoted to greater responsibilities, were the Adjutant General, Colonel Joseph Reed, and the Quartermaster General, Colonel Stephen Moylan. The group was like a real family in the sense that these men were with Washington constantly, and he treated them rather like grown sons, although one or two of them were almost as old as he. He worried about their being overworked, yet he expected them to be on call at any hour of day or night and ready to serve, according to their varying capabilities, as extensions of his own personality. Successful members of this group, which constantly changed its personnel, were likely to become Washington's protégés to a certain extent; and if they left the family for other assignments, Washington wrote them letters which by their candor and lack of reserve showed that he felt tied to them by something more than the formal military relationship.

In many ways Reed was the family's most important member and Washington's closest confidant. Reed had been Washington's first military secretary at Cambridge the year before—a rather surprising appointment because the thirty-three-year-old Philadelphia lawyer had had no previous military experience worth mentioning. He had done well in the job. He was a facile writer who could draft letters for Washington so skillfully that the General needed only to make an occasional correction or insert a phrase or two before he signed them. Reed knew quite a lot about law and public affairs. And Washington, impressed by Reed's suave manner, thought him a first-rate expediter and trouble shooter. When, after four months, Reed had found it necessary to take a leave of absence on account of his personal affairs, Washington missed him so much that he had practically begged him to return, and had finally persuaded Reed to do so by offering him the Adjutant Generalship, which paid seven hundred pounds a year. Reed was now a full colonel and the army's administrative head, and rather inclined to forget, in his natural enthusiasm, that

except for the Battle of Long Island he had had no combat experience at all.

Tilghman, on the other hand, was a most modest
man. He had been on Washington's staff for only a few
weeks, but he had won the General's respect in the
amazingly short time; and Tilghman in turn had been
dazzled by the General, whom he greatly admired.
Tilghman was red-haired, thirty-two years old, and the
son of a well-to-do, well-connected Maryland family,
and he had volunteered to serve specifically as one of
Washington's aides, without pay. He had no commis-
sion. He was not officially recognized in the headquarters roster; he was simply "Mr. Tilghman, acting aide."
But although the position was slightly anomalous, it
made little, if any, difference. Washington regarded
Tilghman as a man of nearly perfect discretion and
talked to him about as freely as he talked to Reed—
ignoring the fact that Tilghman's father was a well-
known Tory and that the young man's brother, Phile-
mon, to whom Tench wrote fairly frequently, was serv-
ing in the Royal Navy. Washington was quite right.
Tilghman was just as reliable as Washington thought
him to be, and there was not the slightest chance that he
would tell too much about what was on the General's
mind, even inadvertently.

Moylan, the oldest member of the group, was thirty-
nine. He was a vigorous, brash sort of man, a past president of the Friendly Sons of St. Patrick in Philadelphia,
where before the war he had been a conspicuously successful businessman. Moylan was capable in many ways,

but for the past two months he had been trying to do more—as both Quartermaster General and a "riding" (as opposed to "writing") aide—than he could manage. He was angry because a good deal of criticism was being directed against him as Quartermaster General. He was willing to agree that the shortages in nearly all categories of supply were terrible, but he had heard just about as many complaints as he could stand. Some of the blame, he felt, belonged to others. He was ready to give up the job as supply chief if Washington wanted him to. But he was not going to let himself be made a scapegoat—and he felt that was happening—without defending himself in a loud, certain voice.

Although Harrison, the chief among the writing aides, came from Virginia, he was not nearly as close to the General, in personal terms, as Reed, Tilghman, and Moylan. Harrison had succeeded Reed in the military secretaryship; and despite Washington's complaint, in a letter to Reed written not very long afterward, that he didn't have a large enough view of things to be really satisfactory, Harrison was a workhorse. He was methodical, a conscientious supervisor and stickler for detail. He seemed able to work endlessly without getting tired. He was clever and he was trustworthy. These were precisely the qualities the job demanded, and it had not taken Washington long to realize that Harrison was not only good but getting better all the time.

The younger men were for the most part personable and promising junior officers. Baylor, Cary, Grayson, and Lewis, Washington's nephew, were Virginia gentlemen. Webb, who came from Connecticut, was the stepson of Silas Deane, diplomatic agent for the Colonies in France. Under circumstances less disheartening than this night's, the spirit of the staff was usually high; and the fairly formal meals, at which the entire group assembled at one large table, were happy occasions. Gibbs, the captain of the headquarters detachment of guards, was the party's comedian. He came from Massachusetts, and with so many Virginia and Maryland accents in the group, he liked to set the table laughing at his exaggerated Yankee colloquial speech.

Now there was no time for anything of the sort. The immediate problem was to dispose the various brigades on the Heights in a defensive formation, trying to make sure that if Howe continued his advance to the north on the following day, Monday, the Americans would be ready to stop him. Washington relied heavily on the advantage of defending high ground, and on the bluffs themselves as obstacles to the hypothetical British attack. They ran east from the Hudson at what is now 135th Street to Point of Rocks, at 127th Street and St. Nicholas Avenue, and then north to the Harlem River at 155th Street. Except for the Post Road draw, three quarters of a mile or so south of the Morris house, there was no way up the bluffs that didn't involve a steep climb—and in some places they were so nearly vertical that climbing was out of the question for soldiers heavily burdened with equipment. Furthermore, Washington could count on his troops being able to see the British

coming, because the ground in front of the bluffs, all
the way around from what was called the Hollow Way
on the west and southwest to the Harlem Plains on the
east, was flat and comparatively open. (The present
125th Street, running east from the Hudson to Morningside Avenue, follows approximately the bottom of
the Hollow Way valley.) As for man-made defenses,
Washington had mapped out three parallel east-west
lines of resistance north of the rim of the plateau—
one at what is now 147th Street, another seven blocks
to the north, and the third seven blocks beyond that,
with the Morris house at its eastern end. Each line was
to be a well-fortified zigzagging series of entrenchments
and redoubts, and the three were to constitute an orderly
defense in depth with the new Fort Washington, a five-
sided, open earthwork, at what is now 184th Street,
well to the rear. But work on the fortified lines had
barely been started. Some of the entrenchments and
three small redoubts in the 147th Street line were complete; the rest of it and almost all of the other two existed only as ideas on paper, with next to nothing actually accomplished on the ground.

There was only one possible remedy—and that was
what Washington's orders that evening specified. He
placed his brigades in rough accordance with the paper
scheme and called on the troops to dig as hard as they
could, concentrating first on the remaining work on the
147th Street line, in the hope that the fortifications could
be improved before the British arrived. Washington
stationed three fresh brigades under General Greene's

command on his southern front, stretched out along the
top of the bluffs between the Hudson and Point of
Rocks. Greene had been sick with the plaguelike fever
for a month and had been out of all the action on that
account; but he was feeling almost himself again, and
the tall Rhode Islander was the most able of Washington's generals. It was clearly a situation that called for
the best commander available, even if his recuperation
was not quite complete. Putnam, with five brigades, was
to stand immediately behind Greene, making a total
of eight brigades in front of the 147th Street works.
And four additional brigades under General Spencer
were on or just north of the line. Putnam and Spencer
were ordered to start their men digging as soon as the
sun rose on Monday. They were to work behind the
protective screen of Greene's troops, with their arms
stacked close by, as long as the British allowed.

If Washington's mind was in any way exceptional, his
strongest intellectual capacity was his ability to see a
situation whole—the quality he had at first found lack-
ing in Harrison. The General was seldom confused by
details. He was not particularly well educated, nor a
brilliant man, but, as Jefferson put it, his mind was
"great and powerful" without being of the very first
order. Washington knew that he could make mistakes in
judgment—that he had done so many times—yet he had
full confidence in his own practical method of analyzing
all the components of a problem, weighing them one at
a time in a systematic manner. After he had defined a

question to his own satisfaction, he was very nearly positive that he at least knew what the problem was. He was much less sure about what to do. Yet sometimes, just because he was convinced that his assessments were right, his solutions seemed extreme—alarmingly bold or hopelessly cautious.

Washington felt himself inadequate in many respects. For instance, he thought that he spoke and wrote badly and that his skimpy training showed in his lack of verbal grace. He was a better writer than he realized. His prose was accurate and lucid to a high degree. He may have been short of felicitous embroideries, so much the style at the time, but he reported skillfully all the essential facts. His writing contained few of the ambiguities that often beclouded the work of his more fluent contemporaries; he chose words and phrases that made his points clearly and simply, and he preferred to repeat himself several times, word for word, rather than cast about for another and probably not quite synonymous phrase. Washington was aware, furthermore, that most Americans overrated his prowess as a general—and on this count modesty had nothing to do with his appraisal. He had learned a good deal in the fifteen months after his appointment and, since he had overcome formidable obstacles of several kinds, his experience suggested that he might be able to overcome others as they arose. Still, the General knew he had been fortunate in starting out with a siege against British-held Boston rather than with an open campaign of formal maneuver. Washington was proud of his Boston success, but the Long Is-

land defeat, underscored now by what had happened at
Kip's Bay, was painful evidence that Howe was his
master at the military set piece, with marching, counter-
marching, and all the other intricacies of drill, fought
on a formal battlefield. Nearly all of Washington's military experience before the war had been irregular,
frontier-style skirmishing in the forests of the Ohio
Valley during the French and Indian War. The military
lessons he had learned then applied only slightly, if at
all, to the present tactical problems. It was true that in
the time since, Washington had acquired a store of useful civilian knowledge as planter, miller, shipper, slave-
owner, legislator, and lay member of the Virginia bench.
And much of what he had learned applied in one way
or another to the job of running an army. But practical
experience at peaceful pursuits could hardly fill in the
gaps in his military training. He was still inexpert at de-
vising strategy on a large scale, and he knew very little
about the conduct of a regular battle, as opposed to
Indian fighting. Subjects like hospital administration
and large-scale recruiting campaigns were new to him,
as was the staggeringly complex matter of supply.

Not long before his appointment to the top command
Washington had imagined that he might be put in charge
of Virginia's troops. In his formal statement accepting
the job of Commander-in-Chief he had said with obvious
sincerity: "I do not think myself equal to the command
I am honored with." He was telling the plain truth.

Washington had agreed to do more than he thought
he could partly because the other candidates, including

Charles Lee, Artemas Ward, and John Hancock, were
also doubtful choices for various reasons, and partly
because he had a strong, almost strange concept of personal obligation. Washington had referred to it in the
letter of June 18, 1775, that he had written to his
wife, Martha, breaking the news of his appointment
and half apologizing to her for having let himself be
chosen:

> My Dearest: I am now set down to write you on a
> subject which fills me with inexpressible concern, and
> this concern is greatly aggravated and increased, when
> I reflect upon the uneasiness I know it will cause you.
> It has been determined in Congress that the whole
> army raised for the defence of the American cause
> shall be put under my care, and that it is necessary for
> me to proceed immediately to Boston to take upon
> me the command of it.
>
> You may believe me, my dear Patsy, when I assure
> you in the most solemn manner that, so far from seek-
> ing this appointment, I have used every endeavor in
> my power to avoid it, not only from my unwillingness
> to part with you and the family, but from a conscious-
> ness of its being a trust too great for my capacity, and
> that I should enjoy more real happiness in one month
> with you at home than I have the most distant pros-
> pect of finding abroad, if my stay were to be seven
> times seven years. But as it has been a kind of destiny
> that has thrown me upon this service, I shall hope
> that my undertaking it is designed to answer some
> good purpose. You might, and I suppose did perceive,
> from the tenor of my letters, that I was apprehensive
> I could not avoid this appointment, as I did not pre-
> tend to intimate when I should return. That was the

case. It was utterly out of my power to refuse this appointment, without exposing my character to such censure as would have reflected dishonour upon myself, and have given pain to my friends. This, I am sure, could not, and ought not to be pleasing to you, and must have lessened me considerably in my own esteem. I shall rely, therefore, confidently on that Providence which has heretofore preserved and been bountiful to me, not doubting but that I shall return safely to you in the fall. . . .

"Censure" and "dishonour"—which now have a rather flamboyant sound—were key words. Washington was deeply concerned about his standing in the eyes of his fellow men. Perhaps his fear of criticism stemmed from doubts he had had early in life about where he stood in relation to the gentry of Virginia, for his inherited position in that society had been second rate. He had worked hard, from about his fifteenth birthday, to raise himself to the topmost level. In accordance with the prevailing custom, Washington's father had bequeathed the best of his considerable lands, the Mount Vernon estate, to the oldest son, Lawrence. The medium-sized Ferry Farm that went to George, the child of a second marriage, was a confusing, betwixt-and-between property, large enough to support a modest, minor planter, but too small to allow anything like the life that Lawrence led as a member of the gentry. Lawrence's education had outranked George's by about the same degree as their inheritances. Lawrence had been sent to school in England, where he had acquired an English gentleman's manner, along with a solid ground-

ing in the classics. Their father had died when George
was eleven, and as a boy he never got to study more
than reading, writing, and arithmetic at schools near his
home and with local tutors. Mathematics was the only
subject in which he showed more than commonplace pro-
ficiency, and when he was sixteen or seventeen, he took a
certificate in surveying at William and Mary.

It was traditional in Virginia that first-born sons
should enjoy immense advantages not accorded to their
younger brothers, and George had not been dismayed
by the difference between Lawrence's upbringing and his
own. It had merely inspired George to try to catch up
with Lawrence, whom he idolized, on his own initiative.
He planned to earn more land and increase the size
of his estate, and his early interest in soldiering was
partly on that account; successful army officers were
often paid for their services in land. He also resolved
to complete his education on his own, reading not Latin
and Greek but history and agriculture; and to try to im-
itate the manners of the first Virginia families, and particularly of the members of the Fairfax family, who
were cousins of Lord Fairfax, one of the greatest land-
owners in Virginia. Lawrence had married a Fairfax,
and the family, who lived near Mount Vernon, had used
its influence from time to time on George's behalf. In
1752 Lawrence died, and Mount Vernon went to
George. Like many others in Virginia at that time, the
farm had been losing money, partly because of the British restrictions on American trade. Washington worked
hard and after a struggle managed to put it on some-

thing like a paying basis; for one thing, he gave up growing tobacco, which was shipped to England, for crops he could sell in Virginia.

By the time he became the proprietor of Mount Vernon, Washington had accomplished most of what he had set out to do; and still he was conscious of the fact that he had worked to gain his position instead of having been born to it, like a first son. That may have been part of the reason why his sense of *noblesse oblige* (a Fairfax hallmark) was so very strong. Washington was literally unable to say no when he was asked, as a gentleman, to take on added responsibilities. He lent money without having it to lend, and went into debt to do so. He was guardian, estate executor, and trustee for a bewildering number of persons, some of whom had practically no claim on his time and energies; and he would spend days in negotiations of the most complicated sort on others' behalf when his own affairs desperately needed attention. In the same way he had been unable to demur when his friends and neighbors picked him for county court judge, or convention delegate, or churchwarden, or anything else that suited the dossier of service of a country squire. He loved the honors that went with his appointments, but sometimes he accepted just because he feared, to use his own word, "censure." He could calmly contemplate death on the battlefield or being hanged as a rebel; what he could not endure was the thought of being accused, justly, of having failed to live up to his obligations.

Once he had made a decision, Washington slept

soundly; in any case, there was nothing at all he could do—after the brigades had been assigned their posts—to influence the following morning's developments. The initiative was entirely Howe's. If the battle was to be continued, and if the American troops lacked the will to fight, as Sunday had certainly seemed to show, then Monday could easily end in a disaster. Yet Washington had insisted on defending the Heights, against the advice of several of his generals, because he put considerable faith in the natural strength of the position. The upper Manhattan ground was not of much use in itself; Washington wanted it only because he thought that with the terrain's help he might be able to win victory there. And that small success, which he had thought necessary before, was more necessary than ever. Without it his dispirited army might melt away entirely and leave Congress with a noble cause and no one to fight for it. But even a token success would require more resolution on the part of his men than Washington was sure they possessed. Yet in some mysterious quarter of his heart, or perhaps their locus was his brain, Washington had remarkable powers of tenacity and perseverance. He took one step and then, if he possibly could, he took the next. If American soldiers were basically cowards, and if Kip's Bay had foreshadowed the loss of the war, Washington was content to wait until Monday to find it out.

V

WASHINGTON got up at about five o'clock on the morning of the sixteenth and, following his custom, worked for a while on his correspondence. He started a draft of a letter to the President of Congress, John Hancock, outlining what had happened the day before. Considering the way Washington had reacted to the sight of his troops breaking and running, the letter's tone was fairly calm, although he did use the words "disgraceful" and "dastardly" to describe their behavior. In concluding, Washington wrote:

> We are now encamped with the main body of the Army on the Heights of Harlem, where I should hope the enemy would meet with a defeat in case of an attack, if the generality of our troops would behave with tolerable bravery; but experience, to my extreme affliction, has convinced me that this is rather to be wished for than expected. However, I trust that there are many who will act like men, and show themselves worthy of the blessings of freedom. I have sent out some reconnoitering parties to gain intelligence, if possible, of the disposition of the enemy, and shall in-

form Congress of every material event, by the earliest opportunity.

Washington turned the rough copy of the report over to Harrison, who was to finish it—some of the sentences were only sketched in—and copy it.

While the General was writing, a reconnaissance party of about a hundred and twenty Americans, commanded by Lieutenant Colonel Thomas Knowlton, was moving south from Greene's front lines, trying to locate the British front on the Hudson River side of the island and to discover—if there were any visible indications—what Howe planned next. The scouts had moved quietly down the bluffs, across the Hollow Way, and up onto the hill south of the Hollow Way—the hill that is now the site of Columbia University, Barnard College, and the Cathedral of St. John the Divine, and that ends on the east in Morningside Heights.

Knowlton and his men were all hand-picked volunteers, members of a new, experimental detachment called "Rangers" which had been organized under Knowlton's leadership right after the Battle of Long Island. There had been such outfits in the American forces during the French and Indian War, led by men like Putnam and Robert Rogers, but Knowlton's group was the first of the kind that Washington had ordered. Light scouting was the Rangers' specialty, but any mission involving more than ordinary danger or requiring more than ordinary individual initiative was likely to come within their scope; they were ready to serve, in the language of their volunteering, "either by water or by land, by night or by day."

One Ranger who was not present, having been put on detached service, was Captain Nathan Hale of Coventry, Connecticut, a Yale graduate who had been a schoolteacher in New London. Hale had been borrowed from Knowlton and been given orders to proceed from the Heights to Long Island, crossing the Sound at the first place where he could find a boat (Norwalk, as it had turned out), to spy on the British. The other men in the detachment did not know what Hale was doing, but the assignment was the kind of mission, beyond ordinary reconnaissance, that almost any one of them might get.

The Rangers had never before been in combat as a unit. They had spent Sunday near Harlem, waiting for the assault that had failed to materialize, and their spirit was so good that they were almost eager for some action. Most of the Rangers came from Connecticut, but there was a scattering of Massachusetts men among them; and most of them were proud that they had been allowed to join the organization.

Knowlton, who was thirty-six years old and a farmer in peacetime, was an authentic hero. He had served with Putnam during the French and Indian War. He had fought in the battle of Wood Creek in '58 and had helped capture Ticonderoga in '60; in '62 he had been in Cuba fighting for Britain against Spain. The greatest day of his military career, however, had been the Battle of Breed's, or Bunker's Hill, where, as a captain commanding the company of Ashford, Connecticut, volun-

teers, he had fought with great courage. Under his
leadership the Connecticut men, with a number of reinforcements, had held a stone-and-rail fence near the base
of Bunker's Hill; and with Knowlton walking up and
down the line, encouraging his troops between pauses to
load and fire his own musket, their stand had foiled
Howe's flanking movement. (In John Trumbull's famous painting, "The Battle of Bunker Hill," Knowlton
is the central figure—the unbelievably handsome young
man in the white shirt with his collar open at the
throat.) He was unusually good-looking. He was six
feet tall, and his deep-set eyes were a striking feature of
his attractive face. And he was a great troop leader: in-
telligent, brave, unostentatious. Knowlton's men idolized
him, and his fellow officers thought almost as highly of
him as his men did. Burr, for instance, had said that "it
was impossible to promote such a man too rapidly."
And Putnam thought that Knowlton was the best officer
who had ever served under his command.

Knowlton and his party, which included both his older
brother, Daniel, and his sixteen-year-old son, Frederick,
had worked their way south, moving cross-country,
toward the British camp. At daybreak, as the Rangers
were moving stealthily through some fields around the
solidly built stone house of a farmer named Nicholas
Jones, which stood on a slight rise that is now just dis-
cernible on 106th Street between West End Avenue and
Riverside Drive, they were spotted by British pickets
guarding the Bloomingdale Road. The pickets immediately fired their guns to give the alarm to the 2nd and

3rd regiments of Leslie's light infantry, which were
bivouacked several hundred yards farther south. Although the Rangers were supposed to be looking for information rather than a fight, they held their ground
when the pickets, from their post at about the present
104th Street and Broadway, took a few ineffectual pot
shots in their direction. The Americans fired several
rounds in return and then took cover behind one of
Jones's stone walls. As they were doing so, about four
hundred British infantrymen, parts of two or three different companies, responded quickly to the pickets' alert
and advanced in column up the Bloomingdale Road.
Knowlton pointed out a spot on the road fifty yards
south of the wall, at about the present 107th Street, and
ordered his men not to show themselves or to fire until
the first soldiers in the British column reached it. The
Rangers did not have to wait long. As the leading infantrymen swung briskly past the mark, Knowlton gave
the order, and his men stood up and fired. The British
formed a firing line. For half an hour the two lines held
their positions, practically face to face, shooting as fast
as they could reload.

The Brown Bess, the English flintlock musket with
which most of the soldiers on both sides were armed,
was a cumbersome weapon. A man firing a Brown Bess
did not aim; he merely attempted to hold his gun parallel to the ground and pointed in the general direction
of his target, and tried to keep from flinching too badly
in the appreciable time interval between pulling the
trigger and the explosion of powder and ball. Even if

he managed to hold his musket perfectly steady, no two
shots followed the same trajectory. The rifle that some
of the Hessian jaegers were using and the long rifles
that some of the Rangers had were both considerably
more accurate—especially the American version, with a
much longer barrel, that was designed to compete successfully with the bow and arrow. To Washington's re-
gret there were only a few long rifles in the whole American army. They were handmade, mostly by Swiss and
German immigrants in eastern Pennsylvania; and although almost every soldier wanted one, their produc-
tion was negligible. An expert long rifleman could hit
a ten-inch target at one hundred yards with fair regular-
ity, and could fire about eight times in four minutes—
almost twice as fast as the average musketman. The time
was saved in loading. A rifle ball was light (weighing
about one ounce) and consequently lacked the punching
power of the heavier musket shot, but because a rifleman used a greased linen or leather patch to hold the
comparatively loose-fitting projectile in place in the barrel, he could ram it home, on top of the powder charge,
fairly easily and quickly. With the lubrication, he needed
to use only a light wooden ramrod for the job. A musketman, on the other hand, needed a heavy steel ramrod,
and sometimes a mallet as well, to drive a musket ball,
which was supposed to fit the barrel tightly, into place.

In the thirty minutes, even with some rifles to bring
up their average, the Rangers managed to get off only
eight rounds apiece. The light infantry's rate of fire was
no faster. The total casualties in the skirmish, mostly

wounded men, came to twenty—ten on each side. The engagement was broken off when, well to the American left and some distance to the east of the Bloomingdale Road, the 42nd Regiment—the Royal Highland Regiment of Foot, commonly known as the Black Watch— moved forward. Its bagpipes were squealing, and its drums were beating out the marching cadence. From the 42nd's direction of movement, Knowlton realized that it intended to outflank his line of Rangers. And since it could easily do so, the Colonel gave the order to retreat.

Except for the Hessians, none of Howe's troops were more feared by Washington's soldiers than the Black Watch, which had fought in America during the French and Indian War. Its men were picked for height—they were all supposed to be at least five feet seven inches tall—and many of them were wild Highlanders, who spoke only Erse. They carried an unusual array of weapons; in addition to their muskets and bayonets, many of them had broadswords, daggers, and pistols. They wore short scarlet coats, kilts, multicolored stockings that came to just below their bare knees, and their famous regimental tartan, a twelve-yard length of cloth which they wrapped around their waists and looped over their left shoulders; in addition, they wore white vests, white goatskin sporrans (a tasseled pouch hanging in front of their kilts), and low, checkered Highland bonnets not unlike berets. The somber colors of the tartans, coupled with their imposing stature, made the men of the Black Watch seem more warlike than any of the gaudy crimson-and-white soldiers of the other regiments.

On Knowlton's order the Rangers fell back, but in a disciplined, orderly manner, taking turns at firing to cover one another's withdrawal. The Black Watch came to a halt. But Leslie's men pursued Knowlton's party as it backtracked along the approximate course of the Bloomingdale Road, using the ground on both sides of the highway in its retreat, as far as the Hoaglandt farmhouse. From there, where the Bloomingdale Road ended, the Rangers continued north—Claremont Avenue now follows about the route they took—into the Hollow Way at about the place the elevated I.R.T. subway station at 125th Street stands today.

Leslie's men were then on a rise known as Claremont, where the Claremont Inn later stood for many years and a few hundred yards north of where Grant's Tomb stands now; they had chased the Rangers for a little more than a mile, and as they caught their breath and watched the retreating Americans moving across the low ground and clambering up the bluffs to rejoin Greene's brigades, the British light infantrymen felt they had done exceedingly well.

The first report to reach General Washington about the Rangers' actions—they were the reconnaissance he had mentioned in his letter to Hancock—arrived at about seven o'clock in the morning, but it had been completely uninformative. Washington had been talking to Reed when a messenger arrived at the Morris house with the cryptic word that musket firing had been heard to the southwest. The men along the 147th Street line had, at first, been alerted. They had stopped the digging they

were doing in accordance with the orders of the night
before, and had taken up their arms; but after a time,
when no signs of a British attack developed, they had
restacked their muskets and had gone back to work on
the entrenchments. Since there was no telling what the
musket fire was all about, and since Reed was eager to
be in the thick of things, he had proposed that he ride
south at once to find out for Washington what Knowlton was doing.

Reed had ridden as far as the Hoaglandt farm. There
he had met and conferred briefly with Knowlton, who
was in the midst of supervising his deliberate withdrawal.
And then Reed had turned around and headed back with a
summary account of the skirmishing and the good news
that even if the Rangers had gone beyond their mission
as intelligence scouts, Knowlton's men had given a fine
account of themselves in the fighting. While Reed was
gone, Washington and some of his aides rode down to
the southern rim of the Harlem Heights plateau, where
the General could see for himself what was happening
on Greene's immediate front.

Shortly before nine o'clock, Reed reported to the General. The Colonel was full of enthusiasm for the showing the Rangers had made, and was convinced that with
a little support Knowlton could do even better. At the
same time Knowlton's men were getting back to their
own lines, and the word was spreading through the
ranks that the scouts had stood up well against columns
of light infantrymen.

It was just then that a British bugler, in the group of

Leslie's men standing on Claremont, in full view of
Greene's right-hand brigade on the bluffs directly to the
north, put his horn to his lips and blew the fox hunter's
signal for the end of the chase, of a fox gone to earth.

The brassy insult was loud, audible all along the top
of the bluffs. It made Reed furious, and he urged Washington to send some men to show the light infantry they
had gone too far. No man among the Americans was
more familiar than Washington with the meaning of the
fox hunter's call, and no one was more eager to try anything that promised a success, but he did not intend to
let the bugler, or Reed, make his decision.

Washington took his time, thinking over the proba-
bilities and working out a limited, practical scheme of
maneuver. He considered whether it was advisable to
force additional fighting. It was not clear, from Reed's
account, just how much support the British were ready
to give Leslie's two regiments; the Black Watch had
moved up, and perhaps others were on the way from the
right or rear. No one knew. On the other hand there
was the consideration which might override all the nega-
tive points: the question of the army's morale. It would
be worth a good deal to win a victory that could bolster
the spirit of the troops. Within a few minutes Washington had concocted a modest plan.

The General did not mean to risk an engagement
with the full British force, whatever it was, nor to try to
drive the British back toward their camp. But he
thought he might be able to lure some of Leslie's confident light infantrymen a little farther north, down from

the high ground of Claremont into the Hollow Way, and then cut them off by sending a strong detachment around to the east, up the rocky Morningside Heights bluff, to their rear. The flankers would have orders to isolate the leading British soldiers by moving in behind them, blocking their line of retreat and standing in the way of any British effort to reinforce them. Two separate, co-ordinated actions would be required: a feint in front of Claremont as if the Americans meant to rush up the hill, which should draw some of the British down into the valley, and simultaneously a stealthy encircling march around the left by a force which would be masked from the British by the terrain and the trees. It was among the most elementary of tactical schemes. On the other hand, it was more, in terms of control and synchronized action, than the Americans had yet pulled off.

Once Washington had made his decision, he issued his instructions fast. Nixon's brigade, the outfit on Greene's right, nearest the Hudson, was to supply one hundred and fifty volunteers for the frontal feint. Nixon chose Lieutenant Colonel Archibald Crary, of Rhode Island, to command the party. And Crary's orders were to make as much noise as possible, as he marched down into the Hollow Way, and to look as if he meant to drive straight ahead up Claremont. Knowlton's Rangers, with three companies from Colonel George Weedon's 3rd Virginia Regiment under Major Andrew Leitch—a total of about two hundred and thirty men— were to make up the flanking group, which Colonel Knowlton would command.

It was not long before Crary's volunteers started
boldly down the bluffs, through the trees, toward Martje
David's Fly, a swampy, salt marsh on the inland side of
a shallow cove at the Hudson River end of the Hollow
Way. (Both Martje David's Fly and the cove have
long since been filled in; if they hadn't, the swampy
ground would reach east almost as far as Broadway between 125th and 130th streets.) There were several
houses, with outbuildings and fences, at the bottom of
the Hollow Way, on the first solid ground east of the
marsh. As Crary's party advanced, a number of the
British soldiers, falling for the feint, ran part of the
way down the Claremont slope, took up positions behind one of the fences and a hedgerow, and opened fire.
The range was too great for anyone to have much
chance of hitting anybody, but Crary's men fired back
and then, continuing to fire, retreated a few hundred
yards in the hope of drawing the British farther north.
At first the British, responding beautifully, moved up a
little, and just so they wouldn't become too optimistic
and attempt to advance too far, eight hundred additional men—all the rest of Nixon's brigade—were sent
down from the Heights to reinforce Crary's troops. The
air was filled with lead, and the firing set up a spectac-
ular racket, but the battle was static; the Americans for
the time being had no intention of pushing ahead, and
the British infantrymen in the valley, greatly outnumbered, lacked the strength to do so. The two forces
simply stood each other off, safely separated by a couple
of hundred yards, and blazed away.

At about eleven o'clock, while the loud, ineffectual firefight continued, Knowlton's flanking party started down from near Point of Rocks—a considerable distance east of the engagement—on its way around to the British rear. Reed, who had just been over the ground, went along to help if he could. The men moved in open ranks, as inconspicuously as possible, heading for a rocky rise on what recently became the site of the General Grant Housing Project, on the block bounded by 123rd and 124th streets, Broadway, and Amsterdam Avenue. From there, the plan was to move stealthily south and west and get in back of Leslie's men. But just as Leitch, who at this point was in the lead, had reached the top of a ledge on the rise, and before the party had started around to the rear, the plan went wrong; someone inexplicably gave the order to fire too soon. And Knowlton's soldiers fired, alerting the British to their presence. The 3rd Virginia was a good regiment—it was a favorite of Washington's, who had known many of its officers before the war in and around Fredericksburg—and the blunder may have been the result of excessive zeal on the part of one of its officers. In any case there was no longer any chance of completing the encircling movement. The British immediately turned and fired to protect their threatened right flank. Leitch was hit three times in rapid succession—once in the hip and twice in the stomach—and was carried to the rear, fatally wounded.

Knowlton immediately climbed onto the same ledge and turned to urge his men to follow him. As he stood

there, in full view of the British, a musket ball hit him
in the small of the back. Captain Stephen Brown, of
Woodstock, Connecticut, who was at his side, caught
him as he started to fall, and asked if he was badly
wounded. Knowlton replied that he thought he was.
Brown was impressed by the fact that Knowlton, despite
the wound, seemed as calm as if nothing had happened.
According to Brown's recollection, Knowlton said, "I
do not value my life if we do but get the day."

Brown took command of the Rangers, and ordered
two men to carry Knowlton to a more sheltered position
—the flanking party was taking a considerable volume
of fire from the British muskets, for Leslie's men had
fully realized that they had to try to stop the attempt to
outmaneuver them. Within an hour Knowlton was dead.

The loss of both Knowlton and Leitch, almost at the
same time, might have been disastrous. The New England and Virginia troops, shocked by seeing their two
top leaders fall, might have lost their nerve, and the four
units in the party could have broken up in confusion. But
nothing like that happened.

Brown and the captains of the three Virginia companies—Charles West, John Thornton, and John Ashby,
Jr.—managed beautifully. The flanking party pressed
hard against the British right. At the same time Crary's
troops stopped shadowboxing and began to attack in
earnest.

Watching from the top of the bluffs, Washington could
see that the fight was going well, despite the flanking
party's failure to get to the British rear. He ordered

Kepp's Bay (1778), by Archibald Robertson. Unfinished sketch, drawn two years after the Kip's Bay landing, with the five British warships penciled in, apparently as an afterthought. (Spencer Collection, New York Public Library)

Kip's Mansion, from *Valentine's Manual.* (1852)
(Courtesy of Museum of the City of New York)

Ruins of Trinity Church, from a sketch by Thomas Barrow (1780). After the fire of September 21, 1776. (Courtesy of Museum of the City of New York)

View of New York taken from one of the redoubts in the rebel lines . . . behind Mt. Pitt, by Archibald Robertson. The city's line of fortifications on the north, with Bunker's Hill on the extreme right. (Harris D. Colt Collection, courtesy of Kennedy Galleries)

View of the North River from the Beach near Lispenards Brewhouse, by Archibald Robertson (10 December 1781). It was on or close to this beach that Captain Bauman found his sail boat. (Spencer Collection, New York Public Library)

View of the North River looking toward Fort Washington, October 16, 1781, by Archibald Robertson. From Claremont, with the Hollow Way and Martje David's Fly in the middle background. (Spencer Collection, New York Public Library)

View across the lower Harlem Valley, looking to the East, by Archibald Robertson. The rugged Harlem Heights terrain, with the Harlem River in the distance. (Spencer Collection, New York Public Library)

View across the upper Harlem Valley, by Archibald Robertson. (Spencer Collection, New York Public Library)

Nathanael Greene, engraved from a portrait by V. Green.
(Spencer Collection, New York Public Library)

General Sir Henry Clinton.
(Courtesy of New York Historical Society)

Admiral Lord Richard Howe.
(Courtesy of New York Historical Society)

General Israel Putnam, by an anonymous British artist.
(Spencer Collection, New York Public Library)

Lieutenant General Earl Cornwallis, by D. Gardner, engraved by J. Jones. (Emmet Collection, New York Public Library)

New York from Brooklyn Heights (6th August 1778), by Archibald Robertson. (Spencer Collection, New York Public Library)

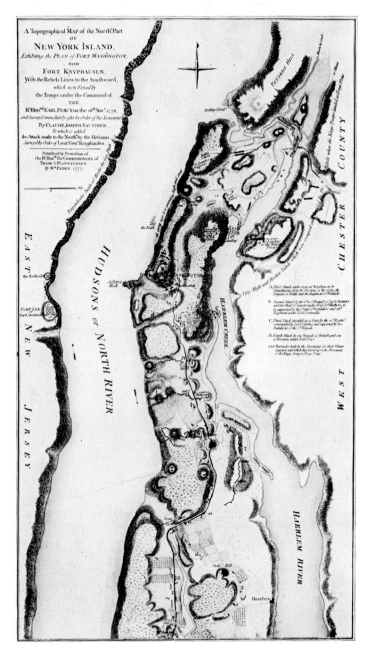

A Topographical Map of the North Part of New York Island, by Claude Joseph Sauthier. Drawn from a survey made immediately after the capture of Fort Washington. (Stokes Collection, New York Public Library)

Forcing the Hudson River Passage (Oct. 9, 1776), by Dominic Serres. A naval action preliminary to the capture of Fort Washington, which shows on top of the high ground on the right. (Courtesy of United States Naval Academy)

A View of the Attack against Fort Washington (16 November 1776), by Captain Thomas Davies of the Royal Regiment of Artillery. From what is now the New York University campus, with the Harlem River in the foreground. (Stokes Collection, New York Public Library)

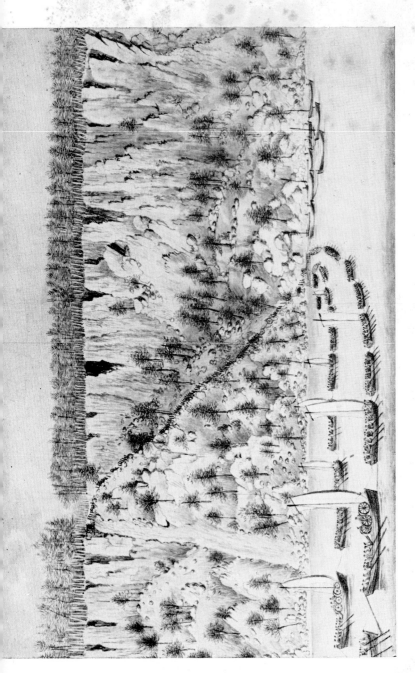

The landing of the British Forces in the Jerseys (20 November 1776), by Captain Thomas Davies. The point of landing was at Alpine, New Jersey, about opposite Yonkers, New York. (Emmet Collection, New York Public Library)

several more outfits, including nine companies of General
Reazin Beall's Marylanders, Sargent's entire brigade,
and Douglas' brigade—the unhappy warriors of the Kip's
Bay fiasco—to move forward and bolster Crary's force.

Leslie's men were no match for such a full-scale attack.
They were forced back from their position, firing spir-
itedly as they withdrew. Instead of backing up onto
Claremont, the way they had come, the British retreated
through the woods along the line of what is now Broadway, backing up a hill, to be sure, but a much less steep
hill, and moving by the shortest way toward their base.
Most of the Americans had never had the pleasure of
seeing the backs of British uniforms, and they were considerably encouraged by the sight. At the top of the slope,
there was a large, open buckwheat field. It covered the
entire crown of the hill, starting at about what is now
120th Street and extending south almost to 116th Street,
and running from Riverside Drive east to Broadway or
a little beyond: it belonged partly to Hoaglandt and
partly to another farmer, Vandewater, whose house was
at what is now 114th Street, a short distance west of
Morningside Avenue. The British fell back, with the
Americans close behind them, until they came to the buckwheat field. On its northern edge, where reinforcements
reached them, they made a stand. Leslie had ordered up
the rest of the 2nd and 3rd battalions and the Black
Watch, and seeing that the Americans were adding to
their strength, he had called for help from Cornwallis'
reserves. Help was on the way: a company of Hessian
riflemen, two small pieces of artillery, the 33rd regiment

of British grenadiers and the Linsingen Battalion of Hessian grenadiers. Leslie's total strength—if all the British reinforcements had reached the battlefield—would have been more than five thousand men.

By this time, which was approximately noon, the engagement had grown far larger than anything Washington had contemplated. A real battle had developed. And although the opposing forces were small, it had become a head-on clash between two formal lines drawn up in regular array. The American line, held by a total of about two thousand men, extended, in terms of present-day landmarks, from the Riverside Church to Teachers College just north of 120th Street. Nixon's brigade was on the right, Sargent's, Beall's and Douglas' men held the center, and Knowlton's and Leitch's party was on the left. The block between 120th and 119th streets, between the two lines, was a kind of no man's land. The British were strung out along 119th Street, or slightly to the south of it.

At first the Americans had a slight but clear advantage, partly because the British were outnumbered. Yet for some time the British line held firm. Leslie's regiments were greatly helped by a pair of brass three-pounders, mounted on wheels, that Lieutenant Wallace of the Royal Artillery and his cannoneers had manhandled all the way to the buckwheat field from McGown's Pass. Each of the guns fired sixty rounds—all of the ammunition the battery had brought with it.

The Americans fought well. Greene, Putnam, Reed, General George Clinton, and several of Washington's aides, elated by the troops' sudden display of courage and aggressiveness, rode back and forth behind the line of musketmen, shouting encouragement. There were still some who tried to run away, and Reed stopped one, a private named Ebenezer Leffingwell, and ordered him back into the line. A few minutes later he again caught Leffingwell beating a one-man retreat, and this time the frightened soldier tried to shoot the Colonel. His musket misfired. Reed seized a musket from another soldier and tried to shoot Leffingwell. This musket, too, misfired. Whereupon Reed slapped the man over the head with his sword and had him arrested. (A week later Leffingwell was court-martialed and sentenced to death, but he was saved from the firing squad when Reed at the last moment interceded on his behalf.) But Leffingwell's case was the exception; on the whole the American units, including Douglas' green brigade, showed an almost unbelievable lift in spirit from their low point, the evening of the day before.

For close to two hours the fight remained virtually a standoff—and then the Americans began pushing the British back. Wallace's battery was almost out of ammunition, and the light infantrymen were low on theirs, and they had not seen fit to attempt a bayonet charge. At about two o'clock Tilghman reported to Washington, who had remained on the Heights, that the British were slowly giving way. The General told Tilghman to order the American commanders to break off the engagement and retreat. Washington did not want his soldiers to go beyond the buckwheat field. He assumed that Howe had

ordered additional strength into the action although
Washington did not know, specifically, that Cornwallis'
and von Donop's grenadiers, who had marched some
three miles at top speed, were nearing the scene of
action.

While Tilghman was riding back to the battlefield with
the order to retreat, the British decided, rather abruptly,
that they had had enough. It was they who retreated,
first into orchards south of the buckwheat field and across
the Bloomingdale Road—back over the ground where
they had pursued Knowlton's party in the morning—and
south in the direction of Striker's Bay. Some of the American soldiers, made reckless by the sight of Highlanders
and British on the run, were taking off after them without waiting for orders. There were brief skirmishes at
about what is now 111th Street, and one, even farther
south, almost to the Jones farmhouse. While the Americans were still in pursuit, the guns of the British frigates
in Striker's Bay suddenly opened fire. The fighting was
too far away and too high above the level of the river
for the guns to do any damage; but their booming was
enough to persuade even the most enthusiastic of the
Americans that it was time to stop.

By then Tilghman had delivered Washington's orders
to the main body of the American force. The men shouted
a "Hurrah!"—as Tilghman reported later—and then
marched back in good order to their camp on the Heights.

VI

Some thirty Americans were killed in the day's fighting. Washington estimated his total casualties, including wounded and missing, at about sixty. In doing so, though, he may have been counting only the most seriously wounded, for the number was probably closer to a hundred and thirty. Howe's casualty figures may not have been any more accurate (like the Americans, the British did their best to minimize their own and exaggerate the enemy's losses), but at least they were not in round figures: fourteen killed and a hundred and fifty-seven wounded. (On the other hand, one of the Hessian officers, Major C. L. Baurmeister, reckoned the British had seventy killed and two hundred wounded.) Whatever the exact numbers were, the Americans had suffered more in one respect: in addition to Knowlton and Leitch, two other officers had been killed, Captain Micaijah Gleason of Nixon's Massachusetts and Lieutenant Noel Allen of Varnum's Rhode Island regiment.

By late afternoon, when the Americans had resumed their defensive positions on the Heights, the men were

talking about the amazing things they had seen during
the day. (In Douglas' brigade, for instance, there was a
story about one lieutenant colonel who had been hit in
the shoulder by grape shot. The missile was said to have
gone through his coat, his vest, and his shirt, but it hadn't
even broken the skin on his shoulder. The only damage,
apart from the holes in his clothes, was to his badly cut-up
epaulet.) Their spirits were so much higher than they
had been only twenty-four hours before that the camp was
hardly recognizable. There was a warm debate, which
could never be resolved, about which outfit deserved the
most laurels. General Greene, who was naturally partial
to the troops from his own state, was greatly pleased by
the way Varnum's and Hitchcock's Rhode Islanders—
both part of Nixon's brigade—had conducted themselves.
Others thought that Leitch's Virginians, or the Rangers,
or the Marylanders, or the Massachusetts men were the
day's outstanding heroes. It was the kind of argument
which troops get into when they are feeling generally
proud of themselves. Even Private Martin, in Douglas'
brigade—which had done a good deal to redeem its reputation—commented, with the understatement of an old
combat veteran, that the sight of the British in retreat
had been "agreeable."

The soldiers' ebullient mood, in contrast to their
despair on the night of the fifteenth, did not reflect any
great satisfaction over having had temporary possession
of the buckwheat field, for it had been relinquished almost immediately, and it hardly mattered (except to
Hoaglandt and Vandewater) who owned it. It was there

for the British to occupy now, if they had cared to do so, but Howe preferred to maintain his left front, as before, in the neighborhood of Striker's Bay. Nor was the lift in morale attributable to the beef ration that was issued—the first food that some of the units had received for forty-eight hours. The real reason for the good cheer on Harlem Heights—as those who had been in the fight were more than happy to explain to those who had manned the defensive lines—was the knowledge that some of the best soldiers in the British army had been forced to run from American troops. The day had proved something that for many of Washington's soldiers had badly needed proving: Howe's impressive regiments, good as they were, could be driven from the field. Speaking of this discovery, Reed said in a letter to his wife, "You can hardly conceive the change it has made in our army. The men have recovered their spirits and feel a confidence which before they had quite lost."

As far as New York's fate was concerned, the change Reed noted was not going to have any important effect. Howe was impressed, and saw that if Washington's troops were prepared to defend Harlem Heights with as much enthusiasm as they had shown on the sixteenth, the cost of a frontal assault on the plateau might be unreasonably high. For the next twenty-six days, consequently, Howe was going to content himself with improvements on his Striker's Bay-McGown's Pass-Horn's Hook line, digging in against the remote possibility of an American counterattack. (But the only real threat to

New York City was fire. Within less than a week, on
September 21st, an all-night blaze burned a large part
of the town to the ground; and afterward it was never
quite as comfortable a place to stay as the British had
envisioned.)

Howe was going to have the upper end of Manhattan,
despite the temporary check to his progress. Instead of
throwing his regiments against the steep bluffs into what
might have been a bitter fight, he would simply outflank
Washington again with another amphibious landing; he
would use his ships to sail past the American position,
land above it in Westchester and, if the Americans
lacked the sense to withdraw after they had been outmaneuvered, he would attack Harlem Heights simultaneously from the rear, the flank, and the southern front.
That was just the way it worked out.

Washington, for his part, was in for a series of defeats
and retreats. He was not only going to lose the rest of
the island but northeastern New Jersey as well. There
was nothing in store for the General but bad news until
he crossed the Delaware and won the battle of Trenton
at the end of December. But even as his army continued
to disintegrate, and most of Washington's worst problems were intensified rather than relieved, there were
going to be repeated demonstrations of the fact—which
the day had already shown—that, under the right circumstances, American soldiers could fight.

On October 12th, for instance, when Howe started to
outflank Harlem Heights by taking a force of four thousand men through Hell Gate with the intention of land-

ing at Throg's Neck (now Fort Schuyler Park in the Bronx, the point of land on the north shore just where the East River joins Long Island Sound), he was stopped by twenty-five well-placed Pennsylvania riflemen under Colonel Edward Hand's command. The Neck was, in effect, an island, connected with the mainland by a bridge and causeway across a creek with marshy banks. Hand's men had taken the planks out of the bridge and had stationed themselves at its far end, behind a long woodpile. When the leading British soldiers appeared, the Pennsylvanians made such a racket and fired so many well-aimed shots in the enemy's direction that Howe's troops abandoned the idea of crossing the bridge. Some tried to cross the creek by a ford, but the Americans discouraged them there, too. The Pennsylvanians were promptly reinforced, and Howe was compelled to stop, encamp for six days, and try again—this time successfully—at Pell's Point (now Pelham Bay Park) three miles farther east.

On October 16th and 18th, in response to Howe's move, Washington fell back to White Plains. He took all but about twenty-eight hundred of his men off Manhattan Island. Those he left were to hold Fort Washington, which they could not possibly have been expected to do; in making one of his worst and most tragic military blunders, the General was again paying too much attention to what Congress, from the distance of Philadelphia, thought wise; and Congress, despite the proof that the captains of the British warships hardly noticed the Fort Lee-Fort Washington line of sunken hulks, still hoped that the barrier might somehow be made to work.

The thirteen thousand or so men in Washington's main army were able to move back, across the King's Bridge and up the west bank of the Bronx River to White Plains; and however cold the comfort may have been, that was in itself more than Washington, on September 15th, had thought possible. The withdrawal was hard. The shortage of wagons and horses was as bad as ever. It took most of four days to finish what should have been about one day's work because the wagons had to make the trip repeatedly, on a shuttle system, and the artillery had to be dragged by hand. Nevertheless the retreat was completed, and although the desertion rate was still appalling, Washington's army did not melt away as it marched.

And on October 18th, while the second part of the army was getting under way for White Plains, there was another encouraging show of American spirit at the village of Eastchester, something more than a mile inland from Pell's Point. Colonel John Glover had been posted there with a small brigade made up of four skeleton regiments, including his own Marblehead, Massachusetts, outfit and three other Massachusetts units under Colonel Joseph Reed, Colonel William Shepard, and Colonel Loammi Baldwin. The entire American force numbered about seven hundred and fifty men. When Howe's four thousand men came on, none the less, Glover's brigade stood its ground. It fought valiantly and for a time forced the British advance guard back until the main body came up. It was a delaying action, and there was no hope that it could develop into anything more. But the Massachusetts men did well, considering their inferior numbers, and the

British were held up in their advance toward White Plains for the better part of the day.

The battle of White Plains, on October 28th, was a defeat for the Americans and it ended in another retreat, but it was neither a rout nor a disgrace. And during the course of the fighting several of the American units— Colonel John Haslet's Delaware regiment, Smallwood's Marylanders, and Lieutenant Colonel Rudolphus Ritzema's Third New York regiment, among others—fought with the greatest gallantry. Perhaps the best testimonial to the quality of the American resistance came from General Howe. He gave up his efforts to get around and behind Washington's army, and to hand it a crushing defeat, and headed back for Manhattan.

And even during the last day of fighting on the island, November 16th, when the British captured Fort Washington, the Americans showed considerable spirit. It was a pointless, shockingly expensive affair from the American point of view. Colonel Robert Magaw, commanding the garrison of about twenty-eight hundred men who were deployed at various points on the Heights with the fort proper as their final point of retreat, had no real chance of holding out against the eight thousand men Howe sent against him. The battle was short, and at the end of it all the Americans, except the sixty who had been killed, were taken prisoner. Two hundred and thirty officers were captured, and the Rangers (by then commanded by Captain Lemuel Holmes), and a precious stock of weapons, ammunition and equipment. There was no real consolation for the disaster. The best that could be said about it was that before Magaw handed over his sword to General Wilhelm von Knyphausen, surrendering the fort in order to prevent the senseless slaughter of the men crowded inside it, Pennsylvania, Maryland, Virginia, and Connecticut men had fought hard and well.

For Monday night, September 16th, however, it was enough that the day had been a rousing success. Nixon's, Sargent's, and Weedon's men, among others, were ordered to retire to quarters to get some rest—and warned, at the same time, that they had better be ready to turn out quickly in case of an emergency. Putnam's men moved into what had been Greene's front-line position at the top of the bluffs overlooking the Hollow Way, and Spencer's took the rest of the perimeter, from Point of Rocks to the vicinity of the Morris house.

Within the next week or so a number of Washington's officers wrote to various correspondents about the improvement they noticed in the American soldiers' morale. "It hardly deserves the name of a battle," Reed said in another letter to his wife, "but as it was a scene so different from what had happened the day before, it elevated our troops very much and in that respect has been of great service."

General George Clinton, writing to the New York Convention, said, "I consider our success in this small affair, at this time, almost equal to a victory."

Colonel Silliman, in a letter to his wife, thought about the effect of the action on the British point of view. "They have found now," he said, "that when we meet them on

equal ground, we are not a set of people that will run
from them. . . ."

Considering how well the small success that he had
planned had produced the effect he had wanted, General
Washington's official report to Congress was a model of
restraint, although it did show some cautious pleasure in
the results. "The affair," he concluded, "I am in hopes
will be attended with many salutary consequences, as it
seems to have greatly inspirited the whole of our troops."

Two days later, on September 20th, Washington wrote
a slightly less formal note to his friend General Philip
Schuyler. He made a statement about his soldiers that
was going to be severely tested over the next seven years,
until at last they re-entered New York. "This little advantage has inspirited our troops prodigiously," Washington wrote. "They find that it only requires resolution
and good officers to make an enemy, that they stood in
too much dread of, give way."

SOURCES

ONE of the school classes the army gives (or at least used to give, fifteen years ago) is called Terrain Walk, or, variously, Terrain Study or Terrain Appreciation. The instructor takes his soldier-pupils out of doors and leads them over some part of the local landscape while he discusses its military significance, pointing out stream-lines, draws, military crests, enfilade, defilade, cover, concealment—and nowadays, probably, helicopter landing areas or 240-millimeter atomic gun sites.

I used to look forward to Terrain Walks whenever they appeared on the class schedule of the several elementary army schools I attended, and it was only partly because they were sessions in which my instructors did most of the work. The transformation of a peaceful South Carolina, Oklahoma, or Maryland landscape into a battlefield, a bivouac, a gas-contaminated area, or whatever, depending on what subject the particular school was trying to drill into me, was almost always fascinating; and, having learned that a meandering brook is a stream-line, perhaps concealing enemy troops if not an ammunition dump, useful in maintaining camouflage discipline

111

but a problem in wire communications, an obstacle to infantry squad movements but a great help, when photo-
graphed from the air, in judging the ground's contours
—and so on, almost endlessly—it has been difficult to go
back to thinking of it, simply, as a meandering brook.

This book started with Terrain Walks that my wife,
Naomi, and I took on Manhattan Island. We were walk-
ing for exercise in the beginning, and our calling our
excursions Terrain Walks was only a feeble family joke.
But the phrase inevitably led to wondering about New
York as a battlefield, and to longer walks, and to the
New York Public Library, the New York Historical So-
ciety, the New York Society Library, and the Museum
of the City of New York (conveniently located on Fifth
Avenue, just a few blocks south of McGown's Pass).

I don't like to think of the walking part of the research
as finished. The fact that so much of the terrain is blan-
keted by buildings, asphalt, and macadam is surprisingly
unimportant; if anything, it adds to the fun of seeing
that the ground goes much as it did one hundred and
eighty years ago. If Sunfish Pond were still in existence,
the bottom end of Park Avenue might be more attractive, but there would be none of the excitement of noting
the low ground—which is still visible—that used to be
the small lake's bed. Kip's Bay and Striker's Bay are still
there; all you need to do is excavate the fill in your mind's
eye. The Hollow Way is especially plain; and to some
extent, at least, it is possible to see nearly all of the ups
and downs of the island that confronted Generals Washington and Howe. Indeed, the smoothing-over effect of
the city's growth almost emphasizes what a hilly island
it was, for not many of its streets and avenues are level

—exactly level, that is—for more than a few blocks at a
stretch. Perhaps the most radical change in our attitudes
that emerged from these battlefield reconnaissances was
what happened to our view of Central Park. My wife
and I have both lived in New York almost all our lives.
Without really thinking about it, we assumed that Central Park had been set aside originally because the terrain
was so rocky and hilly, and so full of lakes and streams,
that no one had been able to think of anything else to do
with the ground. Now we realize, however tardily, that
Central Park landscape is a tidied-up sample of what the
whole island used to be like.

We were helped considerably by some of the volumes
in the City History Club's series of books designed for
terrain walkers, and offering suggested routes. They could
stand updating, because many of the landmarks they
mention are gone. The Revolutionary War buff is not too
badly disappointed, since with the exception of the Jumel
Mansion all the buildings he'd like to see were torn
down ages ago; the trouble is that it is difficult, once
you get walking, to stick to your period, and the Club's
guidebooks are full of reminders of post-Revolutionary
structures, both valuable and charming, that have been
demolished in the past few years.

The starting point for almost all research on New
York is I. N. Phelps Stokes' *The Iconography of Manhattan Island* (New York, 1915–28). *As You Pass By*,
by Kenneth Holcomb Dunshee (New York, 1952), a
book about old New York which is based in part on the
accurate records of the volunteer fire companies, is in-
formative, especially about the lower part of Manhattan.
It puts old landmarks and streets in terms of the present-

day locations with enough care to satisfy anyone. William
Dunlap's *History of the American Theater* (New York,
1832) contains a vivid word picture of the city, recalled
from the author's boyhood. So does his *History of New
York for Schools* (New York, 1837). Stephen Jenkins'
The Old Boston Post Road (New York, 1913) and Alvin
F. Harlow's *Old Bowery Days* (New York, 1931) help
to fix that most important highway firmly on the ground.
While there is no mystery about its location, since the
handsome house still stands on unusually firm foundations
just where it has always stood, *The Jumel Mansion*, by
William Henry Shelton (Boston and New York, 1916),
is a detailed study of the building and its several sets of
interesting occupants. *The Columbia Historical Portrait
of New York*, a beautiful picture book edited by John A.
Kouwenhoven (New York, 1953), contains a number of
the best drawings of New York that were made in the
late eighteenth century, and several of the maps. Except
for the *Ratzer Plan* (London, 1776) and the *Ratzer
Map* (London, 1776), which is reproduced in part on
the jacket of this book, the contemporary maps of Manhattan were mostly charming rather than accurate. Some
of the prettiest among them, drawn more or less free-
hand by British officers as war maps, are wonderfully confusing. On the other hand, the two Ratzer maps, made
from surveys completed a few years before the war, are
both beautiful and true, with engraving so fine that, with
some artistic license, no doubt, the artist shows detail
down to the individual trees in the orchards. It is a pity
that the *Map*, the larger of the two, ends at about what
is now 48th Street instead of covering the whole island.
An Abstract of Title of Kip's Bay Farm, by John J. Post

(New York, 1894), describes Howe's landing area precisely. The New York City Hall of Records, which keeps track of real-estate transactions, is the final authority on geographical fine points, of course; and its mountain of deeds is so well indexed that one can find out who owned almost any given square foot of Manhattan with remarkable ease.

Cities in Revolt, by Carl Bridenbaugh (New York, 1955), has a good deal of information about New York life and culture as well as geography. George William Edwards' *New York as an Eighteenth-Century Municipality* (New York, 1917) tells how the city was administered and governed. *The History of New York During the Revolutionary War*, by Judge Thomas Jones, a fierce Tory account, was published in New York in 1879, carefully annotated by Edward Floyd De Lancey, a collateral descendant of Jones. *Father Knickerbocker Rebels* (New York, 1948) is a more temperate history by T. J. Wertenbaker.

One source book has been important beyond all others: *The Battle of Harlem Heights*, by Henry P. Johnston (New York, 1897). Until Johnston figured out the locations for the actions on September 16th—the route of Knowlton's flanking party and the position of the buckwheat field, in particular—the picture of that day's fighting was hopelessly confused. When he had completed his work, the contemporary accounts nearly all jibed neatly; references in letters and diaries, which had seemed rather muddled according to the pre-Johnston hypotheses, suddenly made sense. In addition to its other virtues, Johnston's book contains more than one hundred pages of documents from American, English and Hessian sources and several excellent maps. Johnston's *The Campaign of 1776 Around New York and Brooklyn* (Brooklyn, New York, 1878) is especially valuable for its account of the Battle of Long Island. *The War of the Revolution,* by Christopher Ward, edited by John Richard Alden (New York, 1952), covers the fighting on Manhattan in just a few pages, but is a wonderfully readable account of the whole war; I have relied heavily upon it. The same is true of Douglas Southall Freeman's *George Washington, a Biography* (New York, 1948–54), John C. Miller's *Origins of the American Revolution* (Boston, 1943) and his *The Triumph of Freedom 1775–1783* (Boston, 1948), a brilliant pair of books, the first tracing the causes of the war and the second the course of the war itself. John C. Fitzpatrick's *The Spirit of the Revolution* (New York, 1924), Bruce Lancaster's *From Lexington to Liberty* (New York, 1955) and J. H. Plumb's *England in the 18th Century* (London, 1950) have been of help. Peter Force's *American Archives* (Washington, D.C., 1837–53), consisting as its full title explains, of a collection of authentic records, state papers, debates and letters, was almost indispensable.

As far as letters and diaries are concerned, my favorite is Joseph Plumb Martin's *A Narrative of Some of the Adventures, Dangers and Sufferings of a Revolutionary Soldier* (Hallowell, Maine, 1830); but there are a great many other valuable contemporary accounts that have been published. Some of those I found most useful were Alexander Graydon's *Memoirs of His Own Time* (Harrisburg, Penna., 1811), *The Memoirs of Major-General William Heath* (New York, 1901), *The Correspondence and Journals of Samuel Blatchley Webb*

(New York, 1893–94), Stephen Kemble's *Journals and Order Books* (New York, 1883–84), Frederick Mackenzie's *Diary* (Cambridge, Mass., 1930), Sir Henry Clinton's *The American Rebellion* (New Haven, Conn., 1954), *Narrative of Sir William Howe* (London, 1781), which is his own explanation of his part in the war, given before a committee of Parliament, and the Marquis de Chastellux's *Travels in North America in the Years 1780, 1781 and 1782* (Paris, 1786). Even though the dates of the last are later than the action I was interested in, the author met and describes several of the people who had been with Washington's army at New York.

For material on the British navy, I've consulted Edwin John Brett's *Illustrated Naval History of Great Britain* (London, 1871), John Charnock's *History of Marine Architecture* (London, 1800–02), Frederick Hervey's *The Naval History of Great Britain from the Earliest Times to the Rising of Parliament in 1779* (London, 1779), W. R. James's *The British Navy in Adversity* (London, 1926) and Alfred Thayer Mahan's *The Major Operations of the Navies in the War of American Independence* (Boston, 1913).

Charles M. Lefferts' illustrated *Uniforms of the American, British, French and German Armies in the War of the American Revolution* (New York, 1926) is the definitive word on this complicated and awkward subject. Others of the details on the two armies and the soldiers in them come from the third volume of *A History of the British Army*, by the Hon. J. W. Fortescue (London, 1902), *The First American Civil War*, by Henry Belcher (London, 1911), Major General

J. F. C. Fuller's *British Light Infantry in the 18th Century* (London, 1925), Archibald Forbes's *The Black Watch* (New York, 1896), Frederick B. Richards' *The Black Watch at Ticonderoga* (Glens Falls, New York, 1910), *The Private Soldier Under Washington,* by Charles K. Bolton (New York, 1902), *Rag, Tag and Bobtail,* by Lynn Montross (New York, 1952), and "Washington and the New Jersey Campaign of 1776," by William Richardson, an article in the New Jersey Historical Society *Proceedings* (Vol. 50, Somerville, N.J., 1932).

Charles Sawyer's *Firearms in American History* (Boston, 1910), T. E. Fremantle's *The Book of the Rifle* (London, 1901), J. B. Brunet's *Histoire Générale de l'Artillerie* (Paris, 1842), and Louis F. Middlebrook's *Salisbury, Connecticut, Cannon* (Salem, Mass., 1935) provided information about weapons, from muskets and pistols to batteries and fieldpieces.

As for the people in this account, and starting with the chief actor, George Washington, I relied primarily on Freeman's monumental work. But a number of other books were valuable, including the biographies of the General by John Marshall (Philadelphia, 1804–07), Jared Sparks (Boston, 1839) and Rupert Hughes (New York, 1926–30), which is not complete. And *George Washington and American Independence,* by Curtis P. Nettels (Boston, 1951), *The Private Life of George Washington,* by Francis Rufus Bellamy (New York, 1951), *The Great Man: George Washington as a Human Being,* by Howard Swiggett (New York, 1953), and Saul K. Padover's introduction to his edition of the *Washington Papers* (New York, 1955). Jared Sparks'

Correspondence of the American Revolution (Boston, 1853) is an interesting collection of letters written to Washington. And *The Writings of George Washington*, edited by John C. Fitzpatrick (Washington, D.C., 1931–44) is the most complete and correct edition of Washington's own writing.

The *Dictionary of American Biography* (New York, 1928–37) and Francis B. Heitman's *Historical Register of the Officers of the Continental Army* (Washington, D.C., 1914) were the starting points, at least, for a large proportion of the other biographical quests; I am not at all sure how researchers managed to survive in the days before the *Dictionary's* bibliographies, at the end of each article, were compiled. Beyond these two invaluable references, however, were *The Lives and Services of Major-General John Thomas, Colonel Thomas Knowlton, Colonel Alexander Scammel and Major-General Henry Dearborn,* compiled by Charles Coffin (New York, 1845), and Ashbel Woodward's *Memoir of Colonel Thomas Knowlton of Ashford, Connecticut* (Boston, 1861), F. S. Drake's *Life and Correspondence of Henry Knox* (Boston, 1873), Noah Brooks' *Henry Knox* (New York, 1900), *Life of Nathanael Greene,* by his grandson, G. W. Greene (New York, 1867), *Stephen Moylan,* by Martin J. Griffin (Philadelphia, 1909), *A Short History of the Kip Family in America,* by Frederick E. Kip (Boston, 1928), *The Life and Times of David Humphreys,* by Frank L. Humphreys (New York, 1917), and *An Essay on the Life and Times of the Honorable Major-General Israel Putnam,* by David Humphreys (Hartford, Conn.,

1788), who was, successively, an officer with Silliman's brigade, Putnam's aide and then Washington's aide.

Memoirs of Aaron Burr, by Matthew Davis (New York, 1837), *The Life and Times of Aaron Burr,* by James Parton (New York, 1857), and *Aaron Burr,* by Nathan Schachner (New York, 1937), were helpful. All give Burr a lion's share of the credit for starting Putnam's column moving north on its escape march; I've been more impressed by the judgment of others (Johnston, for one) who feel that Burr did a fine job without suggesting, on the basis of slender evidence, that he stretched his job as Putnam's aide beyond the point of insubordination—as his ardent admirers insist he did.

The Command of the Howe Brothers During the American Revolution, by T. S. Anderson (New York, 1936), is a solid study of the two British commanders, and *The Life of Richard, Earl Howe,* by Sir John Barrow (London, 1838) and *Sir Billy Howe,* by Bellamy Partridge (New York, 1932) are both interesting. I used William B. Reed's *Life and Correspondence of Joseph Reed* (Philadelphia, 1847) as my principal source on the enthusiastic Adjutant General. William P. Upham's *A Memoir of General John Glover of Marblehead* (Salem, Mass., 1863), Nathan P. Sanborn's *John Glover and His Marblehead Regiment in the American Revolution* (Marblehead, Mass., 1903) and Oswald Tilghman's *Memoir of Lieutenant Colonel Tench Tilghman* (Albany, 1876)—especially the last —were also useful.

There was a time when I thought, innocently, that it might be possible, by concentrating on two small actions

on two successive days on a fairly small island, to find
out all about what happened. As it turned out, to get
even this far, I've had extraordinary help. In addition
to all the walking she has been forced to do, my wife's
research has been at least equal to mine and I have had
her expert editorial advice on all the problems that came
up during the writing. If I could thank her sufficiently,
Naomi would only write "verbose?" in the margin; I
had better not try. And there are a number of others to
whom I am especially indebted: William Shawn, Sander-
son Vanderbilt, and Robert Gerdy, all of the *New
Yorker*; Jeanne Hale and Frances Goldin; Grace Mayer
and Patricia Pulling of the Museum of the City of New
York; Karl Kup and Elizabeth Roth of the New York
Public Library; Meryle Evans of the New York Historical Society; Harris D. Colt; the Kennedy Galleries; and
my editor, Gerald Simons.

B. B., Jr.

INDEX

Allen, Lieut. Noel, 101
American Army, 11; brigade
strength, 30-31; casualties, 15, 43,
65, 67, 88-89, 101, 107; deser-
tions, 16; disposition on 15th, 21-
22, 31; engineers, 11; equipment,
53, 67, 72, 107; infantry drill,
41-42; morale, 15-17, 20, 31, 37-
39, 45-46, 48-49, 63, 65-66, 82, 92,
96-97, 99, 102-3, 106-9; rations,
16, 31, 67, 103; rumors, 39, 54-55,
66; strength, 15-16, 21, 30-31, 51,
59, 68, 98, 106-7; supply, 16, 72,
77; weapons, 29-30, 87-88. *See
also* Artillery; Militia; Muskets;
Prisoners; Rifles; Uniforms
Amsterdam Avenue, 95
Annapolis, Md., 63
Apthorpe, Charles, 64
Artillery: American, 19-20, 29, 54-
56, 106; British, 19-20, 27-28, 37,
58, 97-99; Knox's, 51, 53; Wallace's, 98-99
Ashby, Capt. John, Jr., 96
Ashford, Conn., 85
Asia (warship), 28
Astor Place, 34-35

Baldwin, Col. Loammi, 106
Baltimore, Md., 63
Barnard College, 84

"Battle of Bunker Hill, The," by
John Trumbull, 86
Bauman, Capt. Sebastian, 54-56, 67
Baurmeister, Maj. C. L., 101
Bayard, William, estate, 57
Baylor, George, 69, 72
Bayonets, 36, 42-43, 89
Beachhead at Kip's Bay, 40, 43, 45-
46, 48, 50, 52, 58
Beall, Gen. Reazin, 97, 98
Beekman mansion, 34
Bellevue house, 34
Black Watch, 89-90, 92, 97, 100
Bloomingdale Road, 39, 46-47, 50,
57, 63, 64, 86-87, 89-90, 100; route
of, 35
Boston, 60; siege of, 10-11, 76, 78
Bowery, 34
Breed's Hill. *See* Bunker's Hill,
Battle of
British Army, 9; casualties, 44, 65,
88-89, 101; discipline, 41; formal
drill, 41; strength, 13, 20, 40, 98,
107; weapons, 87-89; 1st division,
40. *See also* Artillery; Hessian
grenadiers; Jaegers; Muskets;
Rifles; Uniforms
British Navy, 9, 12, 15, 19, 26, 59,
61, 71, 100; armament of, 27-28;
and Kip's Bay landing, 26-29, 36-
38, 59; strength, 13, 27-28

123

34TH ST.

Bloomingdale Road

Cross Road

PARK AVE.

LEXINGTON AVE.

THIRD AVE.

BEEKMAN

Corwallis's British Grenadiers and Guards

Murray

Leslie's Light Infantry

Sunfish Pond

The Post Road

Kip

42ND ST.

Watts

Kip's Bay

Stuyvesant's Meadows

Keteltas

EAST RIVER

23RD ST.

Stuyvesant

Newtown Creek

CLINTON'S FIRST DIVISION BEACHHEAD
NOON, SEPT. 15, 1776